In D~~isguise!~~

UNDERCOVER *with* Real Women SPIES

Ryan Ann Hunter

ALADDIN
New York London Toronto Sydney New Delhi

BEYOND WORDS
Hillsboro, Oregon

Ryan Ann Hunter is the pen name for Elizabeth G. Macalaster and Pamela D. Greenwood, who write together.

ALADDIN
An imprint of Simon & Schuster
Children's Publishing Division
1230 Avenue of the Americas
New York, NY 10020

BEYOND WORDS
20827 N.W. Cornell Road, Suite 500
Hillsboro, Oregon 97124-9808
503-531-8700 / 503-531-8773 fax
www.beyondword.com

This Beyond Words/Aladdin edition February 2013
Text copyright © 2003, 2013 by Elizabeth G. Macalaster and Pamela D. Greenwood
Interior illustrations copyright © 2013 by Beyond Words Publishing, Inc.

For information about special discounts for bulk purchases, please contact
Simon & Schuster Special Sales at 1-866-506-1949 or business@simonandschuster.com.

The Simon & Schuster Speakers Bureau can bring authors to your live event.
For more information or to book an event contact the Simon & Schuster Speakers Bureau at
1-866-248-3049 or visit our website at www.simonspeakers.com.

Managing editor: Lindsay S. Brown
Editors: Jenefer Angell, Emmalisa Sparrow
Design: Sara E. Blum
Copyeditor: Michelle Blair
Interior profile illustrations: Jeanette Little
Jacket illustration: David Hahn
The text of this book was set in Adobe Garamond Pro.

Manufactured in the United States of America 0113 FFG

10 9 8 7 6 5 4 3 2 1

Library of Congress Cataloging-in-Publication Data

Hunter, Ryan Ann.
  In disguise! : undercover with real women spies / written by Ryan Ann Hunter.
     p.   cm.
  Includes bibliographical references.
  1. Women spies—Juvenile literature. 2. Espionage—Juvenile literature. I. Title.
  UB270.5.H86 2013
  327.12092'52—dc23
                                                          2012013443

ISBN 978-1-58270-382-4 (pbk)
ISBN 978-1-58270-383-1 (hc)
ISBN 978-1-4422-6726-2 (eBook)

To the women who have worked,
and will continue to work,
unknown and unsung, for freedom.

Acknowledgments

The authors wish to thank the many people who helped with biographical research and locating photos and images.

Pamela would like to thank: Joan Blacker and the interlibrary loan program at the Everett (Washington) Public Library; the research librarians at the Seattle (Washington) Public Library; Connie Sobel, Emma S. Clark Memorial Library, Setauket, New York; Greg Johnson, David Library of the American Revolution, Washington Crossing, Pennsylvania; and EZ Langston, a descendant of Daring Dicey. Special thanks to Harriet Imrey, who provided background on the American Revolutionary War battles and family histories in South Carolina.

Elizabeth would like to thank: Don Wood, Berkeley County Historical Society, Martinsburg, West Virginia; Doris Walters, Medway Institute, Goose Creek, South Carolina; Laird Easton, California State University at Chico, California; John Baldwin, pilot; and Lorna Catling, Virginia Hall's niece. A very special thanks to Maria Gulovich Liu and Jonna Mendez, who took time to share their experiences, review their profiles, and offer inspiration.

BEWARE

— OF —

FEMALE SPIES

Women are being employed by the enemy to secure information from Navy men, on the theory that they are less liable to be suspected than male spies. Beware of inquisitive women as well as prying men.

SEE EVERYTHING
HEAR EVERYTHING
SAY NOTHING

Concerning any matter bearing upon the work of the Navy

SILENCE IS SAFETY

WORLD WAR I POSTER, CIRCA 1914–1918.

Authors' Note

We chose the spies in this book for their daring deeds. Some of their stories were not recorded until long after they happened. We've tried to study all accounts of their lives to make sure what we've included is true, but because these spies worked in secret, all the details about some of their activities will never be known. To make their stories come alive, we've filled in certain scenes with what could have happened in that time and place, being careful to respect the spies and their work.

The spy profile sketches throughout this book were drawn by the illustrator after studying photographs or paintings of the women, found through online research and archives. There are no known references for images for four of the spies: Ann Story, Anna Smith Strong, Laodicea "Dicey" Langston, and Eva Wu. These women were drawn with accurate clothing and hairstyles of the era they lived in to depict a possible likeness to young women of their time.

The past ten years have brought to light more amazing women who worked in shadows. In this new edition, recent research and the release of formerly classified files, enabled us to update the stories of many of the original spies and gave us new spies to share.

Contents

What Would You Do?

O ne of the qualities of a good spy is an ability to adapt quickly if a plan suddenly changes. Each of these spies had to think on her feet:

- **Emily Geiger** convinced a general to send her alone on a two-day ride through the enemy-filled countryside. Caught, she had to think fast to get rid of the letter she carried.

- **Leona Vicario** was hiding in Mexico City after friends helped her escape prison. But the guards were searching for her. She had to make it into the hills.

- **Belle Boyd** discovered a trap set by the enemy. She had to cross an open field between the opposing forces.

- **Louise de Bettignies** swallowed the enemy report written on the grain of rice originally hidden under her tongue. The police saw and gave Louise something to make her vomit it up.

- **Gertrude Sanford Legendre** was steps from the Swiss border when an enemy guard spotted her. "Run," the mysterious man whispered.

- **Eva Wu** looked up from her performance and saw the policemen who had searched her earlier that day. She should have been wearing a red carnation instead of the white, to warn her contact to get away.

What would you do?

Introduction

From the time people started spying—and that's been just about forever—women were part of it. And they were good!

Women dashed through enemy lines, sent secret messages under the nose of the enemy, and led prisoners in daring and dangerous escapes. They went undercover, taking new identities, from apple sellers to crazy neighbors to beautiful stage dancers. Often, it was enough of a disguise for a woman just to be herself. People didn't expect women to have the strength or know-how to be spies.

But they did! Even as young girls, few of these spies fit the mold of a typical girl of their time. They climbed trees, played what were boys' sports, explored the countryside, and even took interest in mechanical things.

A few of the spies were only in their teens when they set out to help the cause they believed in. Young as they were, they weren't afraid to risk their own lives in the wars and conflicts their countries fought. Some were involved in just one mission; others spied—undetected—for years.

The girls and women chose to spy for many reasons: excitement, foreign travel, a career, or a chance to serve their country. Whatever their motives, they weren't content to sit back and let things happen. They were courageous. They were resourceful. They did what they had to do.

The Anglo-Dutch Wars
(1652–1674)

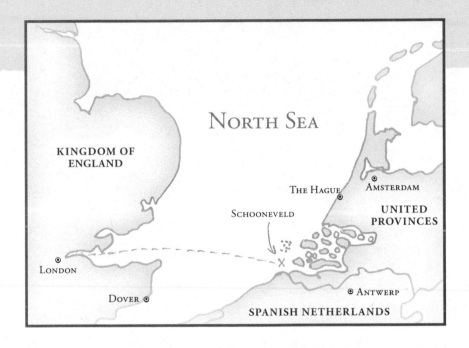

In the seventeenth century, the Netherlands was a peaceful trading nation known as the United Provinces with one of the biggest merchant fleets in the world. The Dutch depended on their strong navy and sea trade to keep their economy stable. They sailed to their colonies in Asia, Africa, the Caribbean, and South America, where they traded for spices, colorful cloth, and exotic plants. The Netherlands became a wealthy empire.

England, also a great maritime nation, wanted these trading routes, but the Dutch refused to make a deal. War was inevitable.

Three wars were fought between the navies of England and the Netherlands. At the end of the third war, England finally defeated the Dutch and gained control of the sea trade. During the second war, Charles II was king of England. While the Dutch had a good spy network, England's intelligence service had become sloppy and ineffective. King Charles desperately needed reliable agents—even if it meant recruiting a woman.

APHRA BEHN

Ahead of Her Time

1640−1689

I must warn the King, Aphra thought after her meeting with William Scot, another spy. Using the cipher code she had learned before leaving on her secret mission, Aphra sent her urgent warning to Lord Arlington:

Beware! The Dutch are planning to sail to England and up the Thames River to sink English ships. You must stop them!

—Agent 169

Aphra Johnson wasn't just any girl. She was born in 1640 in the small town of Wye, near Canterbury, England, and was believed to be the daughter of a barber. As a young girl in the 1600s, Aphra had to follow strict rules. Dancing, card playing, and bright clothing were all banned. Girls were taught to be silent, obedient, and pious. Not Aphra. She was bright, willful, and independent—a girl way ahead of her time.

While other girls embroidered and learned to cook, Aphra devoured books. She was hooked on French romances, which were full of emotion, heroism, and daring. Whenever she could, Aphra also read books

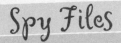

about history, philosophy, and literature—anything that took her beyond her confining life.

Aphra liked to write, and she often composed funny poems. She didn't have a lot of money to buy books, so she copied poems and plays to have her own library. Many girls spent a lot of time on this activity, making quill pens from the feathers of geese and ravens. They drew lines, practiced their letters, and then erased the lines with bread.

At that time, a girl's education might have included some reading, writing, a little math, and music. Aphra also was exposed to foreign languages from the many immigrants who had their hair cut at her father's shop as they passed through Wye.

Early in 1663, Aphra's father was appointed governor of Surinam (now Suriname), a new English colony on the coast of South America, an area where the Dutch were already trading. That fall, Aphra, her mother, father, sister, and brother set sail for the colony. On the way, Aphra's father was killed in a hurricane. Aphra and the rest of her family continued to the colony and lived there for six months. There she met William Scot, a political exile. He had been a spy in the English intelligence service, but had gotten in trouble with the government and had been banished to Surinam.

The following spring, Aphra returned to England. She was already twenty-four years old—nearly too old to get married. Most girls were married by the age of twenty. And if you were unmarried at twenty-five, you were considered a lost cause, a spinster. Aphra had no inheritance, no dowry, and no income. Her only options other than marrying were to become a lady-in-waiting, a chambermaid, or someone's mistress.

Aphra wouldn't consider any of these choices. She wanted to support herself by writing, but this was unthinkable for a lady of that time. Only men earned a living by writing plays and stories. So she married Mr. Behn, a London merchant, originally from Holland. (Not much is known about Mr. Behn, not even his first name.)

The marriage soon ended with Mr. Behn's death from the Great Plague, which ravaged London for more than a year. Merchants were especially vulnerable to this horrible disease, because they couldn't leave their businesses in London. At the time, no one knew that the disease was primarily spread by flea bites, which were more frequent in densely populated areas, so those who stayed in the city died by the thousands.

Mr. Behn didn't leave Aphra much money, and again she found herself in a desperate situation. Then an interesting opportunity presented itself. King Charles II had heard about Aphra's time in Surinam. He was interested in establishing trade with that country, so he asked Aphra to tell him all about it. Aphra eagerly agreed and soon found herself in front of the king, describing all she knew about Surinam—its people, its plants and animals, and how important the colony was to the Dutch.

Aphra was outgoing, funny, and good at mimicking people. The king liked her and invited her to spend more time at his court. With her vivacious personality, her pile of chestnut hair, and decked out in ribbons and pearls, Aphra became very popular.

England and Holland were rivals in trade and had been at war on and off for several years. Although unlikely, a Dutch invasion was possible, and England needed a reliable spy in Holland to keep up with what the Dutch were thinking. The king's intelligence office, headed by Lord Arlington, thought of Aphra. She was tall, attractive, enjoyed socializing, and spoke Dutch. She would make the perfect undercover agent!

William Scot was already in Holland. English intelligence wanted Aphra to persuade William to spy again and reveal any Dutch plots against England. If William agreed, he'd be well paid and pardoned for his earlier mistakes.

How could Aphra turn down such an opportunity? How many other ladies had a job like this? Armed with instructions on how to send coded messages using a cipher, Agent 169 sailed to Holland. She wasted no time in contacting William Scot, who gave her information about the Dutch fleet's plans to attack England.

But despite a steady stream of detailed letters to Lord Arlington, he was indifferent to her. He didn't take her messages seriously, nor did he pay Aphra for her spying. She had to borrow money just to buy food

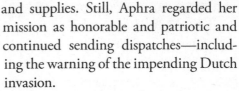

and supplies. Still, Aphra regarded her mission as honorable and patriotic and continued sending dispatches—including the warning of the impending Dutch invasion.

Finally, Aphra got a loan from a friend, and in May 1667, she sailed back to England. She expected to be received at court with praise and back pay. She got neither.

And what of her warning? The king had refused to move on Aphra's intelligence. He believed that the Dutch would never dare invade England. But they did. Not a month after Aphra returned, the Dutch sailed up the Thames river. They set fire to many English ships moored in the river and captured the *Royal Charles*, the pride of the English navy. The English were stunned and humiliated. The war ended in a treaty in which the English gave Surinam to the Dutch.

Aphra tried unsuccessfully to convince the king to reward her for her spying services. Finally, she was thrown in prison for not paying back the loans from her friends. Somehow, she was eventually released; perhaps relatives, friends, or even the king himself, finally paid her debt.

Nearly thirty years old, Aphra was now an ex-spy, a former inmate of debtors' prison, and a widow with no prospect of earning a living. Aphra needed to do something, but she wasn't about to try spying again.

Despite the impossible odds, Aphra Behn became a writer—the first English woman to live by writing. By the end of her life, she had completed more than fifteen novels, seventeen plays, poetry, and translations from French and Latin. In her writing, she created strong, independent, female characters who made their own choices, just as she had.

Aphra's health declined and she was plagued by rheumatoid arthritis. Still, she died pen in hand at the age of forty-nine. She was buried in Poets' Corner in Westminster Abbey.

The Cardano Grille

Invented by Girolamo Cardano (1501–1576), the Cardano Grille was used to send secret messages. Back then, spies made the grille from wood, but you can use cardboard.

To create your own Cardano Grille you'll need:

- Pencil or pen
- Paper
- Two pieces of cardboard the same size as the paper
- Scissors

Follow these steps:

1. Think of a simple message you'd like to send a friend, like "Meet me at the mall 4 o'clock."
2. Cut out word-sized squares or rectangles from different places in each piece of the cardboard. This is your grille. The number of cutouts needs to match the number of words in your message.
3. Place the grille over the paper and write the words in your message in the cutouts.
4. Remove the grille and fill in around your secret message with other words to form a note, part of a homework assignment, etc.
5. Give your friend the note without the grille. Can she read the secret message?
6. No? Now give her the grille to decode your message.

(see example on following page)

The Cardano Grille

STEP #2

meet

me

at

the

mall

4 o'clock.

STEP #3

Hi, Katie: After school I have to meet my mom, who is taking me to the dentist at the corner of the library and Oak Ave. near the mall. I hope it'll be over by 4 o'clock.

Kim

STEP #4

The American Revolution

(1775–1783)

ENGLISH, FRENCH, AND SPANISH SETTLEMENTS IN 1776

☐ = FRANCE   ■ = ENGLAND   ■ = SPAIN   ☐ = UNORGANIZED TERRITORY

For years, the desire for freedom from Britain grew among the colonists in North America. Fighting began in Massachusetts in 1775, and finally, on July 4, 1776, thirteen colonies adopted the Declaration of Independence, proclaiming themselves part of a new country.

The Patriots joined the Continental Army, led by General George Washington. These included settlers homesteading in wilderness areas north and west of the thirteen original colonies. Other colonists, the Tories, remained loyal to the British.

At first, it seemed the British would win the war. They captured New York and Philadelphia. The war spread to the Southern colonies. The Continental Army was not well supplied, and during the harsh winters, many soldiers got sick and died, and others deserted. General Washington sought the support of other countries in Europe. Benjamin Franklin went abroad, eventually convincing France, then Spain and others, to join the Patriots' side.

Women helped on the battlefield. Many got the nickname Molly Pitcher for bringing pitchers of water to wounded soldiers. A few wanted to fight, but they had to disguise themselves as men to do so. Those who stayed home knitted socks and made shirts for the soldiers. They melted their pewter dishes to make bullets. More girls and women than we know dared to spy. They eavesdropped on conversations, gathered information, and carried secret messages directly to the army camps, relying on their wits and courage.

ANN STORY

Standing Her Ground

1741–1817

A nn stood in front of her children, protecting them from the gun pointed at them. Ezekiel, a Tory agent, demanded that she give him information about the Green Mountain Boys. Ann refused, offering only unimportant facts. Ezekiel shouted at her and cocked his gun, threatening to shoot if she didn't give him some straight answers.

Hannah Reynolds was born in Connecticut in 1741. Because she had the same name as her mother, she was called Ann. She and her five brothers were raised with strong Puritan values, and hard work was a part of Ann's life.

In 1755, Ann married Amos Story in Norwich, Connecticut, and they had five children. To improve their lives, Amos and Ann bought a homestead in the British-held wilderness north of Connecticut called the New Hampshire Grants (now Vermont). However, the colonies of both New York and New Hampshire claimed this land. When King George II decided it belonged to New York, the settlers refused to leave or buy their land again. (If settlers had originally paid New Hampshire, they were told they had to pay New York.) The Green Mountain Boys, a local militia, formed to defend the settlers' rights.

The Storys knew hard work, and how to turn their new land into a thriving farm. The family moved to Rutland, and then Amos and their oldest son, Solomon, set out to prepare their home on the shore of Otter Creek near Salisbury. By the spring of 1775, they had finished the cabin and had only a few acres of land left to clear for crops before fetching the rest of the family. They never finished. Amos was killed when a huge maple tree he was felling crushed him.

Ann did not retreat to the comfort of family and friends. Instead, she loaded a packhorse with supplies and a few household items and, with her children, headed to the cabin. She was determined to keep their dream alive.

At that time, battles between Patriots and British troops in Lexington and Concord had stirred the colonies into a full-scale revolution. Many of Ann's new neighbors fled to safer towns farther south. The Green Mountain Boys joined in the fight against the British. The British began arming American Indians to fight with them.

Ann would not leave her home. She supported the Patriots' cause and was willing to risk almost anything to help them.

Otter Creek was an important canoe route, and Ann's home became an outpost for the Green Mountain Boys, a place where they could stop and rest, store ammunition and equipment, and leave intelligence to be passed along.

But the creek was also used by American Indians and Tories. Encouraged by the British army, a party of American Indians traveled down Otter Creek, burning houses along the Grants frontier, including Ann's. When she saw her neighbor's house torched, she hid with her children in their canoe among the brushes at the side of the creek.

Ann knew she couldn't protect herself or her family for long. While they were rebuilding, they'd need a safe place to sleep. With the help of her children, Ann excavated a cave into the far bank of Otter Creek, with extra space to store food and valuables. In the mornings, they returned to their homestead across the creek to work on the cabin and to work the fields.

Her secret cavern was valuable to the Green Mountain Boys, who stored gunpowder and supplies there with little risk of being found. Impressed with Ann's cleverness, the Green Mountain Boys sought her advice. Ann became a trusted spy, reporting on Tory activities.

One evening a Tory agent, Ezekiel Jenny, traveled down Otter Creek toward his meeting with other Tories. He heard a noise coming from underground on the far side of the stream. He remembered that Ann Story's cabin was nearby and suspected he had found an important Patriot hiding place. He knew Ann was an agent of the Green Mountain Boys. The chance to question her was too good to pass up, so he spent the night in the bushes. When Ann and her family emerged the next morning from their hiding place, he followed them to their homestead.

Looking into the barrel of a gun made Ann's heart thump against her chest. But she glared at Ezekiel and calmly told him she wasn't afraid of being shot by a coward like him. He yelled at her again and again, waving his gun. But Ann stood her ground.

Ezekiel couldn't shoot a woman in cold blood in front of her children. He returned to his canoe and continued downstream.

Ann was certain he was up to no good. She tore a page from her Bible, the only paper she had, and wrote a message to warn the Green Mountain Boys. Solomon ran to Middlebury and got the message to Captain James Bentley, a Patriot officer. Bentley formed a posse of Green Mountain Boys, who tracked Ezekiel. They found him and other Tory spies fast asleep in front of a warm fire, rushed in, and captured the entire band.

Because of Ann's warning, the British never received the vital intelligence they needed from the Tory spies for their plan to conquer the Grants region. During the war, rebel soldiers and war refugees continued to find a safe haven at the Story cabin.

In 1791, Ann married a neighbor, Benjamin Smalley, and they moved to Middlebury. When he passed away, she married Captain Stephen Goodrich, also of Middlebury. Ann died in April of 1817.

A cabin has been constructed on the site of Ann's original log home in Salisbury, and a monument there reads: "In grateful memory of her service in the struggle of the Green Mountain Boys for independence."

Spotlight:
NANYE'HI'S WARNING

Nanye'hi hoped for a peaceable solution, as many Cherokee and other American Indian tribes fought against settlements of colonists moving farther and farther into their territory. Nanye'hi, meaning One Who Goes About, was born in 1738. Her mother was a member of the Cherokee Wolf clan; her father, a member of the Delaware tribe. She grew up in territory that became the state of Tennessee.

At age eighteen, she was fighting beside her husband against another tribe, when he was killed. She urged the Cherokee on to victory, and for her valor, she became a Most Honored Woman, one who could vote in tribal councils.

In the early 1770s, skirmishes were not uncommon between her tribe and white settlers. By then she had married the trader Bryant Ward. Nanye'hi, whose name was anglicized as Nancy, sent traders to warn the Overmountain settlements when she learned they were about to be attacked because, she later said, "The same house shelters us and the same sky covers us all." In 1776, she exercised her right as a Most Honored Woman to save the life of a captive, Lydia Russell Bean, from a recent attack. Years later, a grandson of Lydia's married a great-granddaughter of Nancy's.

Concerned the Cherokee would lose their homeland, Nancy counseled her tribe against selling too much of their land to the US government after the American Revolution ended. She died before the Cherokee were made to move farther west.

LYDIA DARRAGH

The Fighting Quaker

CIRCA 1728–1789

L ydia tossed and turned in her bed. She desperately wanted to know what the British officers were discussing downstairs. But what if they caught her eavesdropping? Finally, she could take it no longer. She got out of bed and crept down to the parlor. With her ear to the keyhole, she listened to plans for a surprise attack on General Washington and his troops.

Lydia hurried back to bed, but there was no sleep for her that night. She had to get the information to General Washington. Her son Charles was serving with him. What would happen to him if the British sneaked into their camp? How would she get the message through without getting caught?

Lydia Barrington was born about 1728 in Dublin, Ireland. At age twenty-four, Lydia married a teacher, William Darragh, and they soon set sail for America. After the Darraghs settled in Philadelphia, Pennsylvania, Lydia worked to help support her growing family. She was at various times a midwife, a nurse, and even a mortician. The

Declaration of Independence was drafted in Philadelphia in 1776, and Lydia, in her midforties by that time, believed deeply in independence for the colonies.

When the British invaded Philadelphia, British officers used Lydia's parlor as a regular meeting place to discuss war strategies. The British thought they were safe in her home, since Lydia and her family were Quakers. Quakers didn't believe in fighting or taking sides during wartime. But Lydia had observed the way the British occupiers dined and danced, while many Patriots were sacrificing so much, and came to a different conclusion. Though the British couldn't imagine it, Lydia was a spy, and her oldest son had joined General George Washington's army.

Whenever Lydia heard any useful information, she sent it on to Charles. The night Lydia learned of the British plans for a surprise attack, she resolved to take the news herself. In the early morning, she bundled up in her warmest clothes. Putting her wool cloak over her shoulders, she told her husband she was going to get flour.

The British kept close track of the colonists' comings and goings. The Frankford Mill was about ten miles from town, and women could get a pass to leave the city when they needed flour. Her husband suggested she send their household helper instead, to spare her the trip through the bitter cold, but Lydia said no. She wouldn't even tell him why she was the one who had to go. She would take her chances getting caught, but if the British authorities then questioned her husband, she wanted him to be able to say truthfully that he didn't know anything about it. The British had already hanged several spies.

Lydia took a flour sack and set out over the icy streets. She didn't know how far she'd have to travel. It all depended on whether or not she came across someone she could trust. Sometimes General Washington's soldiers rode about the countryside on horseback to get news from spies, but that meant British cavalrymen were on the lookout, too. If Lydia didn't meet up with a Patriot, she was ready to walk the entire twelve miles to General Washington's camp.

Lydia dropped the empty flour sack off at the mill and then headed for an inn where Colonel Elias Boudinot often met with spies to collect intelligence for General Washington. As she tramped along the road, a Patriot officer who was a friend of Lydia's rode up. She conveyed the information, and he took her to a nearby farmhouse to warm up and eat, while he rode off to pass on the warning.[1]

Because of Lydia's actions, General Washington's troops were ready for the British army's surprise attack. After three days of intense fighting, the British gave up and retreated to Philadelphia, where they spent the rest of the winter.

Lydia was relieved that the battle had gone well, but now she had another worry. What if the British found out what she had done?

Back in Philadelphia, the British

officers summoned Lydia and expressed their surprise that information discussed only in her house had gotten through to General Washington. One of the officers thought she had been asleep the night they were there, because he had to knock several times on her door to tell her to put out the fire and blow out the candles. He looked her right in the eye and asked her if anyone else in the house could have overheard them talking. She was able to say no without flinching. She had waited to answer the door so he'd think she'd been sleeping. No one else had overheard them. She was the only one who had been up that night. They were puzzled, but they did not question her further.

That spring, the British finally left Philadelphia. Lydia continued to help the Revolution by nursing the wounded in the surrounding countryside.

Lydia was later banned from Quaker meetings for going against their practices. It seems she was finally reconciled with them, because she was buried in the Quaker burial ground. At the time of her death, her local newspaper praised her for "her many contributions to her community's health and welfare."[2]

Quakers, a nickname for members of the Religious Society of Friends of Truth, were among the early colonists seeking religious freedom in the New World. But even in the colonies, some Quaker beliefs set them at odds with other Christian denominations and other colonists.

Quakers felt all people were equals—they all had God's "Inward Light" in them. This led many to work as abolitionists, opposing slavery, and to work for women's rights.

This also led them to seek nonviolent ways to settle differences because even their enemies were seen to possess the Inward Light. Standing up for what they believed in led some Quakers to fight against governments and ideas that oppressed people. Labeled Fighting Quakers, they were not welcome in Quaker meetings.[3]

Here are some Quakers you might recognize:

Lydia Darragh became a spy during the American Revolution to work against the British excesses and support the Patriots.

Betsy Ross joined a group of Fighting Quakers to show her support of the Patriot cause. Later, it is believed she sewed the first American flag.

Nathanael Greene was one of George Washington's most trusted generals. It was to General Greene that the spy Emily Geiger (not a Quaker) delivered her message in South Carolina.

Lucretia Mott worked both for the abolition of slavery and the rights of women, before and after the Civil War. Harriet Tubman (not a Quaker) received help and friendship from Lucretia, and Harriet joined her in speaking out for women's rights.[4]

ANNA SMITH STRONG

Spy in Petticoats
1740–1812

If the British were watching her, Anna hoped they would think she was just hanging her wash out to dry that sunny morning on Long Island, New York. Little did they know a petticoat on a clothesline could be a secret signal. And Anna's was!

Anna Smith's great-grandparents were early settlers in Setauket, Long Island, New York. Anna was born on April 14, 1740, in the manor house her great-grandfather built when he first arrived in the colonies. When she was twenty years old, she married Selah Strong and they started their family in the manor.

Many of Anna's wealthy relatives were Tories, but Anna and Selah were Patriots. Selah served as a minuteman when the Revolution first broke out. After the British took over New York City and Long Island, he was arrested and held in a British prison ship under miserable conditions.

Selah was released after Anna begged her Tory relatives to intervene for him. But he wasn't safe in Setauket. The British had even taken over the manor house. Selah fled to Connecticut, which was still in Patriot hands, taking his and Anna's younger children with him. Anna was determined to stay on Long Island, because she was a spy.

General George Washington needed a way to get information about what the British were planning, where their troops were moving, what ships were bringing supplies to them. He set up a network of spies, called the Culper Ring, to carry information on a complex route, from New York City to Setauket, across Long Island Sound to Connecticut, then on to him. There was danger of messages being intercepted at every point, but Anna's help made the transfer of information a little easier.

Most of the spies in the ring were Anna's childhood friends, whom she knew she could trust. Her immediate danger lay in keeping the British from being suspicious of her.

About once a week, one of the spies rode to New York City to dig up information about the British troops. Upon his return, he would hide the message in a wooden box buried on Anna's friend Abraham Woodhull's farm, across the bay from her. Meanwhile, Anna waited for word from another spy, Caleb Brewster, who had been a whaleboat captain and knew the waters well. He would slip past the British ships and hide in one of the coves in the bay.

Once Anna found out where Caleb was, she hung out her black petticoat. That meant Caleb was ready. The spies had given all the coves a number, so beside the petticoat she hung up the corresponding number of handkerchiefs. Three handkerchiefs meant "go to cove number three."

Abraham kept a close watch on Anna's clothesline. He would count Anna's handkerchiefs and know exactly where to find Caleb. This saved him from stumbling around looking in cove after cove, which would have made it easier for the British to figure out he was up to something. Under cover of darkness, Abraham sneaked across the fields right to Caleb's hideout.

Once Caleb got the message, he rowed over to Connecticut and got it to the spymaster. From there it went straight to General Washington.

One day, the British got hold of a letter General Washington had written about a new spy in the ring. Luckily for Anna, the spies in the ring had code names, and most of the messages were written using code words. But the new spy didn't have a code name yet. He was found out. Other members of the Culper Ring grew increasingly concerned about their safety.

Their service had been invaluable to General Washington for nearly four years. As the Culper Ring became less active, Abraham sent a message directly to General Washington with news that the British were ready to cease the fighting, and he thought that independence would be offered to the colonies. Official news of this didn't reach General Washington for several months.[1]

After the war ended, Anna was reunited with her husband and their children. They moved back to the family manor house. Years later, Anna had the honor of meeting General Washington, president of her new nation, the nation she risked her life to help create.

A Dead Drop

The moment when undercover agents meet each other to exchange information is extremely dangerous. The wrong person might see them and figure out what they are doing. So, many spies hide messages in prearranged secret places called dead drops. A dead drop can be a hollowed-out rock or log, or just an unexpected place, like the pages of a book in a library.

To make your own dead drop, mold papier-mâché or craft clay into the shape of a rock or garden decoration to hide outside. Make sure to leave part of the inside hollowed out for the message.

Let the dead drop dry and then paint or decorate it to fit in where you plan to hide it. Use oil-based paints or add one or two coats of varnish to help make it waterproof. If you are going for the natural look, roll it in dirt, sand, and barkdust when it is still a little sticky. Will it look like other rocks in a garden? Will it be kitschy yard art? Insert your message. Will it be written in code?

Once the dead drop is in place, give a friend the prearranged signal that there's an important message waiting for her. Make a game of it by timing how quickly she can find it, read the message, and do the task.

EMILY GEIGER

Caught!

CIRCA 1762–1790

*E*mily *knew she couldn't outrun the Tory scouts who blocked her way. So she pulled up her horse and answered their questions. She told them she lived on Cedar Creek, almost twenty miles away. They were sure she wasn't just out for a ride and accused her of being a spy.*

They locked her upstairs in a farmhouse and went to get a woman to search her. Emily paced back and forth. The message she carried was sure to be found!

Emily Geiger was born about 1762 in the Fairfield District of South Carolina. Her father was a well-to-do plantation owner. Emily and her family were Patriots. But many of the residents of the area were Tories. It seemed everyone was spying on everyone else.

Eighteen-year-old Emily kept up with all the war news even though her father was too old to fight. The war in the southern colonies was going badly for the Patriots. General Nathanael Greene and his troops attacked the British at Fort Ninety-Six, but the British were too strong for them and they had to retreat. After marching for several days, General Greene set up camp near Emily's plantation.

Emily overheard one of the Patriots telling her father that General Greene was looking for a fresh horse so he could send a message to General Thomas Sumter, who was camped farther east. The British had divided their own forces and would soon be on the move again. The Patriots might be able to surround one portion of them if General Sumter's troops could join up with General Greene's troops in the low country.

Emily was tired of hearing all the bad news. She wanted to do something to help. She knew the area so well she felt she could ride through it blindfolded. She could surely take the message faster than any of General Greene's weary soldiers.

Reluctantly, her father agreed, and Emily galloped to General Greene's camp. He must have been shocked when he discovered she wasn't just bringing him the horse but was offering to take the message herself. He didn't want to send her into danger. Tories would be patrolling the area, on the lookout for anyone heading toward General Sumter's camp.

Emily laid out her plan. She knew the roads well, and she had family along the route. It would be easier for a young girl to get through than for a Patriot soldier.

Her confidence convinced General Greene she could do it. Hurriedly, he told her the details as he wrote down the message. No matter what happened, he warned her, the enemy must not see the letter. He couldn't protect her if she were caught.

Emily rode more than halfway to the camp when the Tories stopped her. Not believing her story that she'd traveled alone for two days just to visit nearby family, they locked her in an upstairs room of a farmhouse.

Trapped, Emily peeked through the window. A Tory woman strode across the field right toward her. Emily was about to be searched! There was only one thing to do.

Emily read over the letter, and then tore it up. Piece by piece, she ate it. When the woman arrived to search her, nothing could be found.

Back on the road, the next time she was stopped, it was by General Sumter's men. She boldly relayed the message to them. Then Emily and her horse were able to rest as the soldiers prepared to meet the British.[1]

LAODICEA LANGSTON SPRINGFIELD

Daring Dicey
1766–1837

*D*icey *didn't dare ask anyone for help. Her father had already warned her to be extra careful after some of their neighbors saw her spying on the British. But when she learned the settlement where her brother was staying would soon be attacked, she had to do something to warn him.*

Later that night, when everyone was asleep, she sneaked out of the house and headed for the river. She plunged into the rough water, swift and swollen from recent rainstorms. Tugged by the swirling current, she barely made it across. Dripping wet, she hurried on and reached her brother before dawn. She warmed herself by his fire, and then quickly headed back home, hoping her brother and his friends would get away in time.

Dicey was Laodicea Langston's nickname. She was born May 14, 1766, to Solomon and Sarah Langston, who owned a plantation in South Carolina. Dicey's parents were Patriots. The Langston family prospered, working hard to raise and harvest their crops. Dicey was strong and spunky. She worked alongside her older brother on the plantation, and she missed him enormously after he joined a company of Patriot fighters.

Dicey's neighbors were almost equally split between Patriots and Tories. Because the British were being beaten by General Washington's army in the northern colonies, the British turned their attention to the southern colonies and won many battles. Though it was dangerous, Patriot soldiers roamed the countryside in small bands like the one Dicey's brother joined. They would not let go of freedom without a fight.

The Bloody Scout was the name for a group of Tories known to be especially cruel to the Patriots. They were also the ones who were planning to attack the settlement where Dicey's brother was. They'd threatened Dicey on several occasions because they suspected her of carrying information to the Patriots. After her nighttime trip to warn her brother, they paid her father a visit. Dicey heard them shouting as she came in from the fields. They said they'd shoot her father on the spot if he didn't tell them what he knew. Dicey ran to him and threw her arms around him. She told the men they'd have to shoot her first.

Suddenly, one man pushed the gun aside and told them not to shoot. The men left without harming Dicey or her father. The Bloody Scout had an agreement among them. They would show mercy if one of them asked for his neighbors or relatives to be spared. That day the Langstons were lucky.

Dicey's bravery didn't stop there. On another occasion, her brother sent his friends for a musket he had hidden at home. He told Dicey to ask them for a sign so she'd know it was them. When they arrived, Dicey ran to get the musket. Only when she brought it out did she realize she'd forgotten to ask for the sign. Immediately, she demanded it, but one of the men just laughed—he had no need for a sign; the musket was in reach.

Dicey pointed it right at him, daring him to take it. He quickly gave the sign, admiring her nerve. Several years later, this young man, Thomas Springfield, returned to ask Dicey to be his wife. After the war, they settled in the area and raised many children, grandchildren, and great-grandchildren.

When Dicey died in 1837, the local newspaper praised her for her "many daring deeds on behalf of her suffering country and friends."[1]

PATIENCE LOVELL WRIGHT

Artist and Spy
1725–1786

Trouble awaited Patience Wright one evening as she walked through Paris. The tall, athletic woman was stopped by guards who demanded to see what was in the bundle under her arm. She was furious. Her olive-green eyes flashed as she protested, loud and flamboyant as ever. The guards insisted that she open the bundle. They stepped back in horror. Inside was a human head!

Patience did not speak French and could not understand their conversation, but she could see they were intent on arresting her. She repeated the name of the hotel where she was staying, "Hôtel de York, Hôtel de York," until they took her there. A friend at the hotel explained that Patience was an artist.

How the officers laughed when they discovered the head was one of her waxwork figures! But Patience had another use for her artwork. Her hollowed-out wax busts concealed secret messages. She was a spy for America.

Patience Lovell was born on Long Island, New York, in 1725. Her family moved to a small town in New Jersey when Patience was four years old. Her father had some odd ideas. He insisted that the entire family dress in pure-white clothing to symbolize their innocence and cleanliness. Patience and her eight sisters worked and played in white flowing dresses, white veils, white straw hats, and white wooden shoes! Her father believed in the value of artistic expression, though. So the girls put color into their lives in other ways. They played with clay and flour dough. Patience especially showed a talent for sculpting miniature figures. The sisters learned how to mix pigments and painted the figures in brightly colored clothing. They acted out stories with the figures.

Patience couldn't wait to grow up. Her family's farm overlooked the Delaware River, and perhaps ships and travelers going to and from Philadelphia sparked her imagination. Perhaps the arts drew her there. When she was old enough, she left home for Philadelphia, about twenty miles away. She tried to make a living as a clay modeler, but she didn't have much success. She discovered she liked to travel, and she made friends easily wherever she went.

At age twenty-three, Patience married Joseph Wright and they settled in her hometown to raise a family, though she was soon left alone to provide for her young children when Joseph died. Her sister Rachel, also a widow, had a great idea: Waxwork shows were popular throughout the colonies. Why not try their hand at wax figures? The sisters agreed to start a waxworks business, which over the years turned into a great success. They each established galleries—Rachel in Philadelphia, Patience in New York City.

Patience made busts of several well-known American statesmen. While she was traveling in Boston, she met Ben Franklin's sister, Jane Mecom. Jane offered to write a letter to introduce Patience to Ben, who was in London. He could introduce Patience to famous people there who might pose for her.

So in 1772, Patience set sail for London. When she met Ben Franklin, Patience had a surprise for him, a little trick she had perfected in New York City. As she sat chatting, she worked with her hands hidden under her apron to shape the head of her host. Ben was startled to see a perfect replica of himself. He was amazed by her talent.

Patience settled in the posh section of London near Buckingham Palace. She opened her doors, and men and women of society came in glittering waistcoats and velvet gowns. Patience wore only a plain homespun dress, but she was bold and brash. The British were captivated by her. Over and over she told the story of the nine little girls in white growing up in New Jersey. Her waxwork was praised in London newspapers. Lords and earls sat for her. Even the king and queen sat for her and, to their bemusement, she insisted on calling them George and Charlotte.

Then the Boston Tea Party took place across the ocean. The British lords passed what the colonists called the Intolerable Acts. People in England were divided. Many felt the punishment for the colonists too harsh. Others felt the opposition in America had to be crushed.

Patience chatted casually with her patrons as they posed for her, asking questions about the colonies. Then she sent letters to leaders in the colonies, telling them which people in London they could trust and what the British military was planning. When she discovered letters sent to the colonies were being intercepted, she devised another way to send news—tucked into the hollowed-out wax busts she sent to her sister's gallery in Philadelphia.

While in England, Patience took every opportunity to speak out for American independence and to encourage those back in the colonies to fight what she considered to be British oppression. When she heard about the battles in Massachusetts at the start of the Revolution, she marched down to the palace and scolded the king!

At this time there were many rumors of plots against the king. Some Americans were imprisoned in the Tower of London. Patience worked for their release and gave refuge to prisoners who escaped, helping them get to safety in France.

As the colonists in America started winning battles, Patience continued to speak out. She was threatened by the king's men and went to France for a while. Waxwork was gaining popularity there, and she was able to continue her work.

When the war ended, Patience was back in England. Her son Joseph, who was also an artist, went back to America to do a portrait of the triumphant General Washington. Patience, now in her sixties, began making plans to return to America, but she fell before she could leave, and she died from injury-related complications.

If she had returned, Patience surely would have met General Washington. When she wrote to Washington to thank him for sitting for her son, he replied: "I should be proud to see a person so universally celebrated; and on whom Nature has bestowed such rare and uncommon gifts."[1]

The Wars of Independence in Spanish America
(CIRCA 1810–1838)

COLONIAL AMÉRICAS

Spaniards settled throughout the Americas during the same time period the British colonized parts of North America. Though the Spanish colonies were separate from each other, their social structure was similar. Spanish-born citizens had the most privileges and held the highest offices. Criollos, who had Spanish ancestors but were born in the colonies, and American Indians seemed to be second-class citizens. Small groups, mainly Criollos living in larger cities, met in secret to study the independence movements in the United States and France. They, too, wanted freedom.

Wars throughout Spanish-held America were fought separately in the various colonies over decades. Present-day Mexico was part of New Spain. In 1810, Padre Hidalgo, a parish priest in the small town of

Dolores near Mexico City, raised the cry for freedom from Spanish rule, the *grito de Dolores*. Though he and other leaders of the revolution were executed, those fighting for independence would not give up.

Present-day Colombia was part of New Granada. In 1810, Criollos forced the viceroy of Santa Fe (now Bogotá) out. A civil war began among the various groups of revolutionaries to determine who would govern. At one point, Spain took control again. After years of fighting, the revolutionaries joined forces under General Simón Bolívar and won their freedom.

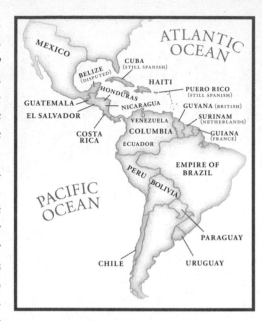

POST-COLONIAL AMÉRICAS

Women did their part. They helped support families whose sons and fathers were fighting. They raised money, and wealthy Criollo women even spent their own fortunes to buy supplies for revolutionary soldiers. Some women spied, and some had to go into hiding in the hills because of their beliefs. Women were not afraid to die to win freedom for others.

JOSEFA
ORTIZ DE
DOMINGUEZ

La Heroina
1768–1829

The lock clicked. Josefa's skirts swished as she marched across the room to look out the window. As soon as her husband left the house, Josefa called to the guard, who supported the revolutionaries as she did. Being locked in her room was not going to stop her from warning the revolutionary leader, Padre Hidalgo, that the Spanish authorities were looking for him.

Josefa's husband was the corregidor, *the top royal official in town. He was ordered to conduct a search for the revolutionaries and their spies. He sympathized with them, but he wanted to stay on the good side of the viceroy. And he wanted to keep his wife safe.*

Josefa, however, wasn't worried about her own safety. She would do anything to help Mexico be free from Spanish oppression. Through the keyhole, Josefa urged the guard to warn Hidalgo with the news. But when the guard reached Hidalgo, the revolutionary leader refused to go into hiding. Instead he rang the church bells in his parish, calling the people to start the revolution against Spain.

Josefa Ortiz was born in a small town outside Mexico City in 1768 to a Criollo family. Josefa's parents died when she was very young, and she grew up in a school founded to educate orphans and widows.

Josefa had to work for her education, and she made the most of it. When she graduated from college, she married Miguel Dominguez, a young lawyer she met when he visited the school on business. When he was appointed *corregidor* (mayor), Josefa was suddenly at the center of social and cultural activities. But she didn't sit back and enjoy a privileged life. She had washed dishes and scrubbed floors at school. She knew what it was to be poor, and she knew the laws in the country were unjust.

Josefa joined a group of leaders and intellectuals who were dissatisfied with Spanish rule. They met in secret to discuss how to fight for freedom. Many Mexicans longed to be free from Spanish control, and they put their hopes in Padre Hidalgo and his uprising.

Spanish authorities began hearing rumors of the coming revolt and questioned Josefa's husband about weapons they thought were hidden in a baker's house. He knew the weapons were hidden elsewhere, and the revolutionaries would not be exposed if he led a search of the baker's house. While they searched, the revolutionaries would be able to get away. Before he left, he locked Josefa in her room. He knew only too well she would try to help, and might get herself arrested. He wanted to keep her safe. She still managed to send the message to Hidalgo, whispering through the keyhole to the guard, who headed out himself.

Several days later, both she and her husband were arrested. Leading citizens came to their defense, and finally they were released. Josefa, though closely watched, refused to stop working for the revolutionaries and started spying as a way to stand up for her beliefs.

Josefa sent the revolutionaries information about government activities the way people today write anonymous letters: She cut words out

Spy Files

Who wants to touch poop?! That's why fake tiger doo made such a good hiding spot for messages in the Vietnam War.

of publications and pasted them together. She rolled up the notes and wrapped them around firecrackers. No one thought to inspect firecrackers for secret messages.

Josefa convinced townspeople and even soldiers in the viceroy's army to join the independence movement. She gave money to aid the revolutionaries and once again fell under suspicion. The viceroy sent an official to question her. Leave it to Josefa. She didn't pass up any chance to spread her beliefs. The official reported back to the viceroy that Josefa had even tried to recruit him!

This time when Josefa was arrested, she went straight to prison. As she was led through the streets, she reprimanded the soldiers: "So many soldiers to guard one poor woman? Well, with my blood I will create an inheritance for my sons."[1]

Josefa did not have to shed her blood. She was not executed, but she was placed in solitary confinement, because she would not stop giving speeches to everyone around her.

Eventually, Josefa was let out of prison to care for her ailing husband. A new viceroy offered peace to the revolutionaries, letting them take over the government. Josefa did not wholeheartedly approve of what was happening. She accused some of the revolutionaries-turned-rulers of gaining power for themselves and ignoring the poor, for whom the war had been started.

Years later, Josefa was honored by the Mexican state legislature for her role in the struggle for independence. Today, a statue of her resides in the Plaza de Santo Domingo in Mexico City, commemorating her work.

A Skytale Cipher

Ancient Greeks invented the skytale (rhymes with *Italy*), which was a stick wrapped with narrow strips of papyrus, leather, or parchment. The message was written on the wrapping, then the strip was removed and passed to the messenger. To avoid detection, a leather strip could be worn as a belt. Only when the strip was rewound around a stick with the exact same diameter as the original could the message be deciphered.

To create your own skytale, you'll need:

- Rounded stick (wooden dowel, broomstick handle, or paper towel roll)
- Paper
- Tape
- Pencil or pen

Follow these steps:

1. Cut two or three one-inch-wide strips of plain 8½" x 11" paper, and tape them together to form one long strip.
2. Tape one end of the strip at a diagonal at the top of the stick and wind the rest down in a spiral.
3. Write a message across the stick, placing one or two letters on each section of paper, depending on the spacing.
4. Unwind the paper and give it to a friend with instructions on how to decipher your message. Be sure to tell her the exact diameter of your skytale.

LEONA VICARIO

Madre de la Patria

1789–1842

The mass ended, and Leona and two of her friends left the church. It was a pleasant day, so they strolled to the market-place where vendors sold fresh fruits, vegetables, and brightly colored dahlias. Suddenly a woman none of them knew stepped into their path and handed Leona a note. She disappeared as quickly as she had come.

Leona's blood raced as she read the message: "The courier is in jail. The authorities are looking for you." [1]

Her spying had been discovered! She managed to stay calm and continued walking with her friends. A short distance away, she hailed a coach and asked to be taken to a small village on the outskirts of Mexico City. From there, she walked to another village. For the next three days, she moved from house to house, while her friends in Mexico City were questioned as to her whereabouts.

Knowing she could not go back, Leona found someone to guide her and set out for the camp of the revolutionaries, hidden in the sur-rounding hills. There she would be safe.

Leona Vicario was born in Mexico City on April 10, 1789, to wealthy Spanish-born parents. They were well educated and made sure their daughter received good schooling, even though at that time, girls in Mexico often received only religious training.

Leona was beautiful, and she was smart, too. She studied classical literature, the history of Mexico, natural sciences, philosophy, French, music, drawing, and painting. Many intellectuals in Mexico discussed how citizens in other countries fought for their freedom, and Leona soon came to support Mexico's desire for independence from Spanish rule.

When Leona was only eighteen years old, her parents died suddenly, and one of her uncles became her guardian. He helped her set up a home of her own and let her control the substantial fortune her parents had left her. She met a young lawyer named Andrés Quintana Roo at her uncle's law firm. Andrés shared Leona's beliefs about the independence movement. When he asked Leona to marry him, her uncle, who supported Spanish rule, refused to give his consent. Leona bowed to her uncle's wishes, and Andrés left Mexico City to work for the revolutionaries.

Leona encouraged others to join the revolution, saying she wished she were a man so she could fight with them. She organized all the best arms makers in Mexico City to journey to Campo de Gallo, where the revolutionaries were hiding. This was a huge blow to the Spanish government and a great help to the revolution. Leona paid for weapons and other resources. She believed so deeply in the cause of freedom that when her money was gone, she began selling her silver, jewelry, and furniture.

Leona also set up a spy ring, the Guadalupes, sending couriers to rebel camps with information about what the government in Mexico City was doing and where their troops were being dispatched. Enriqueta was Leona's code name, and she used other code names for other revolutionaries. But when one courier was intercepted, government officials figured out it was Leona who sent the message. They were planning to arrest her the day she received the warning in the marketplace. The day after her daring escape from Mexico City, she was declared guilty of treason.

Because her uncle was loyal to the government, he convinced the officials to give Leona a pardon. He sent out a search party to find her. At first she refused his help, but she wasn't used to life on the run. She eventually returned to Mexico City. When she wouldn't cooperate with the government officials, they arrested her. No matter how much they threatened her, she wouldn't reveal the names of other revolutionaries.

After she spent forty-two days in prison, Leona escaped with the help of her friends and family. She hid in the surrounding neighborhood. Dressed as a ragged mule driver, her face streaked with dirt, she escaped from the city again.

She met up with Andrés, and this time when he asked her to marry him, she accepted. Many of the leaders of the independence movement were caught and executed, and Leona and Andrés spent several more years in hiding. Their first daughter was born in a cave in the hills. They kept speaking out in favor of independence and freedom for the poor, refusing all offers of pardon from the government.

When the revolution finally ended, Leona dedicated herself to the care and education of her two daughters. She wished to receive no special honors, saying her service was nothing out of the ordinary. But she has been honored throughout Mexico. At the time of her death, the government newspaper called Leona *Madre de la Patria*, mother of her country.

Finding Family Stories

What do you know about the women in your family? Many women's stories are lost because their contributions to history haven't always been valued by our society, and the women themselves don't always realize what they've done is important enough to record. We only know about some of the early spies in this book from stories they first told to their friends or relatives. Fortunately, Lydia Darragh told her daughter Ann. And Emily Geiger told her cousin Elizabeth. Both mentioned their stories to trusted friends, who passed them down. This kind of knowledge is often the starting point for historians in their research.

Talk to your mother, aunts, and grandmothers about courage—the kind of courage the girls and women in this book displayed. Ask about the courage they've shown at home, in school, at work, or in special circumstances in their lives. Ask them what they remember about their grandmothers and great-grandmothers.

Write down their stories, filling in the information about birthdates and places and parents, what they studied in school, where and when they graduated, if and when they got married, and the names and birth dates of their children. Add photographs and keepsakes.

Who knows? You may find an unsung hero in your own family. You are sure to find girls and women who have done amazing things.

POLICARPA SALAVARRIETA

La Pola
1795–1817

*The soldiers closed in around La Pola. She had been caught at last.
Her thoughts were not on her tragedy but on the papers hidden in
the kitchen—papers filled with the names of all the others in her spy
ring. How could she destroy them before the soldiers began searching
the house?*

*La Pola started shouting at the soldiers, calling them cowards
and praising the revolutionaries. She turned to Andrea, the young
mother who owned the house, and said that the baby needed to be
fed. Andrea immediately understood what La Pola wanted her to do.
Andrea hurried to the kitchen, and La Pola kept the soldiers distracted
with her ranting and raving. Soon all the papers were burning in the
kitchen fireplace.*

Policarpa Salavarrieta, nicknamed La Pola, was born on January 26,
1795, into a Criollo family in Colombia.[1] She grew up in Guaduas,
a stopover on a major route between the coast and Santa Fe (now
Bogotá), the capital where the viceroy lived. Her father was a merchant,

and the family lived two blocks from the central plaza—a perfect spot to hear news carried by the travelers. La Pola often knew what was happening in the outlying areas before the viceroy did.

The young girl was at the center of it all. She listened to the grumblings of Criollos who were tired of being under Spanish rule. Two of her older brothers were Augustinian monks. The head of their monastery was a staunch believer in freedom for the colonies from Spain. La Pola read all the pamphlets he wrote in support of a revolution.

She was fifteen years old when a small group of Criollos took over the government. While other Criollos remained loyal to the Spanish rulers, La Pola cheered the revolutionaries who marched through the streets, wishing she could join them. She was full of courage and always ready to speak out. La Pola talked young men into joining the battle for freedom. She helped families whose sons were fighting. When revolutionaries captured by the loyalist soldiers were chained together and paraded through the village, she gave them sips of lemonade or coconut soup.

Most important, La Pola became a spy. She moved to Santa Fe and joined a circle of several other women who supported the revolution. She was a seamstress and worked for wealthy Spaniards, making clothing for them in their homes. She eavesdropped on their conversations and learned such things as where the Spanish troops were moving and what they were planning next.

The Spanish troops managed to retake the government, and a reign of terror began. Revolutionaries and anyone suspected of supporting their cause were executed. Many who were opposed to Spanish rule now fell silent, but not La Pola.

La Pola organized couriers who delivered information to the wealthy Almeyda brothers. Supplying money and arms, they led an uprising as Simón Bolívar gathered his forces. More and more young men joined in the fight. They escaped into the *llanos*, grasslands beyond the city, using a network of safe houses La Pola set up.

One of the Almeydas' contacts turned traitor and revealed their identities. The Almeydas were imprisoned, but that didn't stop La Pola. She continued sending messages and supplies to the revolutionary camps. Then a courier was caught carrying a note from her. The Spanish authorities found out who she was and began a relentless search for her.

La Pola was not ready to go into hiding. Not yet. She had one more escape to plan. With her help, the Almeyda brothers broke out of jail and disappeared into the *llanos*.

A few days later, one of the shopkeepers she knew took a bribe and betrayed her. Soldiers burst into Andrea's home. La Pola was taken to jail. She could save herself—all she had to do was give up the names of others and she could go free.

She refused. And she refused to be silenced in her support of the revolution. Even as La Pola was led through the streets to be executed, she cried out: "Although I am a woman and young, I have more than enough courage to suffer this death and a thousand more. Do not forget my example."[2]

People did not forget her example. Many others lost their lives fighting for independence in Colombia. But independence came. Today La Pola is honored as a national heroine.

The Civil War

(1861–1865)

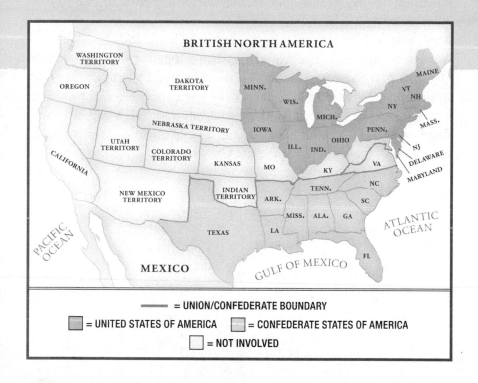

BRITISH NORTH AMERICA

WASHINGTON TERRITORY

OREGON

DAKOTA TERRITORY

MINN.

WIS.

MICH.

MAINE

VT

NH

NY

NEBRASKA TERRITORY

IOWA

PENN.

MASS.

UTAH TERRITORY

COLORADO TERRITORY

OHIO

ILL.

IND.

NJ

DELAWARE

CALIFORNIA

KANSAS

MO

KY

VA

MARYLAND

NEW MEXICO TERRITORY

INDIAN TERRITORY

ARK.

TENN.

NC

SC

MISS.

ALA.

GA

ATLANTIC OCEAN

PACIFIC OCEAN

TEXAS

LA

MEXICO

GULF OF MEXICO

FL

——— = UNION/CONFEDERATE BOUNDARY

■ = UNITED STATES OF AMERICA   ■ = CONFEDERATE STATES OF AMERICA

□ = NOT INVOLVED

Not one hundred years after the United States gained independence from Britain, war broke out within the country itself when Confederate forces fired on Union-held Fort Sumter, South Carolina. But unrest had been growing in the United States for years over the issue of slavery. While there were no laws against slavery, more and more people were speaking and acting out against it.

When Abraham Lincoln was elected president, many Southern states expected slavery to be outlawed. They wanted each state to have the right to govern itself on this and other issues. Eleven states voted to secede. Together they formed the Confederate States of America and elected Jefferson Davis as their president, setting up their White House in Richmond, Virginia. The remaining states fought to preserve the Union.

Women were active in all aspects of the war. A few marched on the battlefields as flag bearers, but those who wanted to fight had to disguise themselves as men, as they had done in the American Revolution. Men thought women shouldn't even be on the battlefields as nurses, but women insisted. At home, women gathered together to roll bandages and pack baskets of food for the soldiers. Women, including slaves and former slaves, were in position to see the war happening around them; to learn valuable intelligence about troop movements, weaponry, and supplies; and to pass information along. One of the best networks operating during the Civil War was set up by a woman.

HARRIET TUBMAN

Without Equal
CIRCA 1822–1913

*H*arriet tied the scarf under her chin and shuffled along the dirt roadway. She looked just like an old slave woman taking the chickens to market. Along the way, she whispered to the slaves she knew. Tonight she would be waiting in the woods to lead slaves out of the South and into the North.

As she turned a corner, she sucked in her breath. One of the masters she had worked for was coming toward her. He might see through her disguise! She had to get away from him. Quickly she loosed the cords that held the chickens. He laughed as the squawking chickens flew over a fence, but he kept on walking when Harriet chased after them, stumbling and waving her arms.

Harriet got the last laugh. That night, several slaves escaped with her to freedom in the North.

Harriet Ross was born on the eastern shore of Maryland around 1822. Her parents, Harriet Green and Benjamin Ross, told stories of their parents' lives in West Africa, among the Ashanti tribe of warriors. Harriet herself seemed to have a warrior spirit.[1]

Her birth name was Araminta, Minty for short. Eventually, she changed her name to Harriet after her mother. It wasn't legal for slaves to go to school, so Harriet never learned to read or write. Harriet's owner, Mr. Brodess, hired out his slaves to work on his neighbors' plantations. From the time she was five or six years old, she lived on other nearby plantations, working long hours even though she was very young.

One time when Harriet was setting the table, she reached for a taste of sugar when her mistress's back was turned. She'd never had it before, and it looked so good. Her mistress caught her and beat her so hard that she spent weeks at home under her mother's gentle care. Harriet got a reputation as being uncooperative, and other mistresses refused to hire her, so she was sent into the fields. She was only five feet tall, but she developed strength driving oxen and splitting logs to make fence rails. Harriet often worked side by side with her father, who showed her the North Star and told her how to use it like a compass so she'd never get lost.

When she was about fifteen years old, Harriet tried to protect a slave from a beating. As the slave broke free, the overseer threw a heavy lead weight at him and hit Harriet's forehead instead. She was in a coma for weeks, and for the rest of her life she was subject to sudden blackouts and severe headaches. As Harriet recovered, once again under her mother's care, she began to think about the nature of slavery. Didn't slaves have the right to liberty, too?

Harriet married a free black man, John Tubman. Even though he was her husband, he threatened to turn her in if she attempted to run away from her owner. But Harriet couldn't stop thinking about the injustice of slavery. When she was younger, two of her sisters were sold to plantations in the deep South. In 1849, after Mr. Brodess died, his wife sold one of Harriet's nieces. Harriet decided she would never let that happen to her. She convinced her brothers to run away with her. Tramping through the cypress swamp in the dark of night, her brothers worried that they'd never make it, that they'd end up getting lost or being caught by the overseer and receiving a terrible beating. Eventually her brothers stopped and refused to walk any further. Harriet returned with them.

When she crept back into bed that night, she knew next time she wouldn't give up. Next time she'd go alone. Several days later, as darkness fell, Harriet set out on the path she would take many more times over the years, leading other slaves to freedom. After hiding during the days and trudging night after night, she finally stood on free soil in Pennsylvania. "I looked at my hands," she recalled later, "to see if I was the same person now that I was free." As the sun warmed the fields, she thought it was how heaven must feel.[2]

Soon after that, Harriet started the work she was most famous for, being a conductor on the Underground Railroad, the secret network of blacks and white abolitionists who helped slaves escape to freedom in the North.

Over a ten-year period, Harriet led some seventy slaves to freedom. No one who went with her ever got lost. Up North, she supported herself as a cook and a maid in local hotels. Despite the danger of her own capture, again and again she went back for brothers and sisters, their spouses and children. Her father insisted he remain in the South to help others escape, but when she found out he was about to be arrested, she went to

Spy Files

The Underground Railroad started soon after slaves arrived in the colonies and became more organized before the Civil War. Safe houses were located along routes leading north. Legend has it that Freedom Quilts might have marked safe houses, draped over a porch rail or used as a window covering.

get him and her mother. They weren't strong enough to travel that distance on foot, so she rigged up a horse-drawn carriage. Eventually her parents and other relatives settled with her in Auburn, New York. She tried to convince her husband to leave the South, too, but he had taken up with another woman. Harriet felt both hurt and angry, but continued with a new resolve to do her chosen work.

Authorities offered a $12,000 reward for Harriet's capture. When war broke out, her friends hurried her off to Canada. Unable to stay hidden when there was work to be done, Harriet went to South Carolina to assist blacks who sought refuge with the Union forces. As the war progressed, the Union officers relied on information about Confederate plans to better prepare for battle. They knew about Harriet's work slipping secretly through the countryside on the Underground Railroad. Could she help them now?

Harriet took on a new mission: to be a spy. She organized a small band of black men to act as scouts, searching out where the enemy stored food, ammunition, and livestock and reporting on the location of troops. For two years she spied on the Confederates. Union officers, recognizing her intelligence and courage, asked her to lead a raid on South Carolina's Combahee River. In several gunboats, she and Union soldiers headed upriver to destroy bridges and ammunition. On the way back, many Confederate plantations were burned and rice crops were flooded. The gunboats picked up some 750 slaves along the riverbank and carried them to freedom.

Harriet's old head injuries started causing her serious problems. She returned to her home in Auburn for a while, and was on her way back to South Carolina when the war ended.

After the war, Harriet supported herself and her parents by working in her garden and selling vegetables and apples. She raised funds to start schools for blacks in the South. She learned her husband, John Tubman, was killed in a race riot. Even after marrying her second husband, Nelson Davis, Harriet was known by the famous Tubman name.

Harriet gave speeches for women's rights with Susan B. Anthony and other suffragists. She believed that no one—woman or man, black or white—would be truly free until everyone was free. She nursed sick neighbors and eventually started a home for aged and impoverished blacks. She moved into it herself a few years before her death.

England's Queen Victoria was so impressed when she read a biography of Harriet that she sent Harriet a silver medal commemorating Victoria's Diamond Jubilee. Harriet was not awarded any honors by the US government for her service but, following her death, the citizens of Auburn recognized the significance of her life's work and set up a bronze memorial plaque at the courthouse in her honor.

William Still, an antislavery activist who worked with Harriet on the Underground Railroad, wrote of her courage, her cunning, and her tireless work: "She was without equal."[3]

ELIZABETH VAN LEW

Crazy Bet
1818–1900

The coded message was ready. Crazy Bet hid it in her basket and headed for the marketplace, humming in her crazy way. Hiding behind a silly smile, she scanned the crowd, looking for one of the spies she knew could take the secret message to the Union officers.

Suddenly a strange man whispered in her ear as he passed. "I'm going through tonight!"

Crazy Bet quickened her pace to catch up with him. She wondered if she should slip him the message. Then she wondered if he really was a spy for the Union. He might be a Confederate detective. They were swarming around the city looking for spies.

As she glanced at the man's face, something told her to keep walking. She hurried home, hoping she could find another way to send the message.[1]

Crazy Bet is what people started calling her, but her name was Elizabeth Van Lew. She was born into one of the wealthiest families in Richmond, Virginia, on October 15, 1818. Her father owned a successful hardware business. Her mother came from a prominent family in Philadelphia, where her grandfather was once the mayor.

The Van Lews lived in a huge mansion and kept a staff of slaves. They entertained famous people, including poets and politicians. Jefferson Davis, the man who became the president of the Confederacy, was a frequent guest in their home.

Elizabeth was as delicate as a china doll. Curly blond hair framed her face. When she was seven years old, Elizabeth went away to her mother's former school in Philadelphia, where attitudes against slavery were strong. Elizabeth was the kind of girl who thought things through for herself. It didn't matter if she was from the South, she realized, because she did not believe in slavery either. After she finished her studies and returned home, she dared to speak out against slavery, even at her father's parties. Her friends were shocked, but that didn't stop her.

When Elizabeth was twenty-five years old, her father died. Over the next few years, both her sister and her brother married and left home. Elizabeth wasn't eager to marry, and she decided to take a lengthy European tour. She wanted to get away and see what the world had to offer. When she returned home, Elizabeth talked her mother into freeing all their slaves. Many of them stayed on to work for pay, because the family had never mistreated them.

The disagreements over slavery tore the country apart. Several southern states seceded. Elizabeth wasn't the only Virginian who wanted to stay in the Union. She attended the debates in the legislature. Tempers were hot, and those in favor of secession threatened to harm those who opposed it.

Finally, the legislature decided. Elizabeth watched in horror as the Confederate flag flew over Richmond. Even if Virginia was now part of the Confederacy, Elizabeth was determined to stick to her beliefs. Alone in her garden, she made her life-changing decision: She would continue to speak out against slavery; she would be loyal to the Union, not the Confederacy.

One hundred years earlier, Elizabeth's great-aunt Letitia had aided colonists imprisoned by the British during the American Revolution. Perhaps inspired by the family stories of Letitia's daring, and because she knew how much Civil War prisoners were suffering, Elizabeth decided to help Union soldiers imprisoned in an old warehouse near her home.

In many people's opinion, Elizabeth was helping the enemy. Friends stopped calling on her and her mother—they were outsiders now, branded Union sympathizers.

Elizabeth started spying on her own. As she visited the Union prisoners, they told her about battles and troop strength. Young men from all over the South poured into Richmond, which had become the Confederate capital, to join the Confederate army. The Union prisoners paid attention to all this. They only knew bits and pieces, but Elizabeth was sharp. Listening to the bits and pieces, she began to see the big picture of the war.

At first, Elizabeth wrote letters containing strategic information and mailed them directly to Union officials. Then she wrote to General Benjamin Butler and offered to spy for him. Her understanding of war maneuvers impressed him, and he accepted. Just one thing: He wanted her to send messages in secret, not through the mail. So Elizabeth set up her own spy ring. In case her couriers were caught, she had created a cipher to encode the messages—she used a combination of two numbers for each letter in the alphabet.

Because the Van Lews owned a farm just outside of Richmond, the people who worked for Elizabeth had passes to go in and out of the city. Messages were often placed in a few hollowed-out eggs, hidden among intact eggs in a basket. There were other Union spies operating in Richmond, but the Union generals considered Elizabeth's spy ring to be the best.

At night sometimes, Elizabeth herself delivered messages to a Union spy who sneaked into the city past the Confederate guards. To disguise herself as a poor farmhand, she dressed in stained work clothes, stuffed her cheeks with cotton, and wore an old

Spy Files

The Civil War marked the first time hot air balloons were used for military reconnaissance. An observer in this high-tech spy gear could telegraph intelligence from one thousand feet high about a camp three miles away.

sunbonnet. No one recognized her as she rode her horse through the dark streets to her secret meetings.

Eventually it dawned on the prison guards that Elizabeth spent a lot of time talking to the prisoners. They wanted her visits to stop. That's when Elizabeth adopted her best cover. She went about town with her hair all mussed up, her clothing mismatched, talking, humming, and laughing to herself. The guards decided she couldn't really have a serious thought in her head. People who used to respect her called her Crazy Bet, Bet being a nickname for Elizabeth, as she passed by.

Spy Files

Crypto-*what*?

Cryptogram: Something written in code or cipher.

Cryptograph: A device for writing or solving cryptograms.

Cryptography: The art of writing or deciphering messages in code.

Whenever Union prisoners escaped, they knew to head for the Van Lew home, where Elizabeth would hide them in a secret room under the eaves. Her neighbors spied on her and reported her to the Confederate officials. Elizabeth's home was searched to no avail, and she was often followed. More than once, Confederate detectives tried to trick her into revealing that she was a spy for the Union. But she seemed to have a sixth sense about it. She never got caught.

Elizabeth grew frightened as she read about Union spies being captured and hanged. She didn't lose her courage, though. Her work was too important. When the Union General Ulysses S. Grant set up camp outside Richmond, messages from Elizabeth's spy ring flew back and forth. When he wanted to know about the strength and location of the Confederate defenses, he sent messages to her. He knew he could count on Elizabeth to find out.

Finally General Grant's troops were able to break through the Confederate defenses. Confederate President Jefferson Davis announced that the army would leave Richmond. Many people from the city crowded onto trains and buggies, trying to flee. But not Elizabeth Van

Lew. Overjoyed, she raised a smuggled-in Union flag of stars and stripes over her home.

Elizabeth spent much of the family fortune helping prisoners, bribing guards, and taking care of her spies and household workers. After the war, she gave her money to organizations to aid and educate freed people. When General Grant became president, he honored Elizabeth by appointing her postmaster of Richmond. But the people of the South never forgave her. Her former friends and neighbors simply ignored her. Elizabeth compared living in postwar Richmond to the feeling of traveling in Europe where she couldn't understand the foreign languages.

Elizabeth was not reappointed as postmaster after President Grant was voted out of office. She became impoverished and wrote to some of the families of veterans she had helped when they were prisoners during the war. Grateful for what she had done for them, the families collected money and sent it to her.

At the end of her life, Elizabeth was lonely but said she would have done it all again. She didn't understand why people couldn't forgive her. She wrote in her journal that she was called names for being loyal to her country: "Here [in the South] I am called 'Traitor,' farther North a 'Spy,' instead of the honored name of 'Faithful.'"[2]

Spycraft:

Elizabeth Van Lew's Cipher

The cipher Elizabeth Van Lew used substituted two numbers for each letter in the message. Only people who had the key to the cipher could read it. Elizabeth kept this cipher key folded in her watchcase.

Can you decipher this message?

14434354124366

(Hint: Be sure to separate the numbers into pairs first, starting with 14.)

6	R	N	B	H	T	X
3	V	I	U	8	4	W
1	E	M	3	J	5	G
5	L	A	9	0	I	D
2	K	7	2	Z	6	S
4	P	O	Y	C	F	Q
	1	**3**	**6**	**2**	**5**	**4**

Here's how it works:
To find the letter that 14 represents, locate the number 1 in the vertical column at the left of the grid. Then locate the number 4 in the horizontal row at the bottom of the grid. Now, with your eyes or fingers, trace across the row the number 1 is in, and trace up the column the number 4 is in. The letter in that box is G.

Find the letters represented by the other pairs of numbers in the same manner. Now you've got the message!

Share the grid with a friend and send messages back and forth in Elizabeth's code.

MARY
BOWSER

From Slave to Spy

CIRCA 1839-?

A s the Davis children entered the dining room for dessert, smiles
and gentle laughter replaced the adults' frowns and talk of war.
*The new servant, Mary, took the opportunity to glance at a paper one
of the officers had carelessly placed on the side table. There were notes
from the latest battle. As she scanned the page, she memorized every
word. She had been listening to the war talk as she served the platters
of Virginia ham, roast turkey, and oysters.*

*Suddenly Mary got that prickly feeling you get when you know
someone is staring at you. She turned and saw Mrs. Davis frown-
ing at her. Mary calmly, but quickly, picked up bowls of pudding,
bowed slightly to the Confederate First Lady, and served dessert to
the eager children.*

*She sensed the danger of being caught even though her disguise
was perfect. No one would expect a former slave to be able to
read, let alone understand anything about troop strength and war
strategy.*

Mary Bowser was a former slave, but she was not uneducated. Born about 1839, she was baptized Mary Jane Richards in the Van Lew family's church and grew up in their Richmond, Virginia, household.[1] When Elizabeth Van Lew returned home from school in Philadelphia in the late 1830s, there were lively discussions at family parties about slavery. Elizabeth spoke out against it. Mrs. Van Lew quietly agreed with her daughter. Mr. Van Lew didn't agree, but he treated Mary and his other slaves with respect.

After Mr. Van Lew died in 1843, Elizabeth and her mother freed their slaves. Then they asked Mary the most startling question: Now that Mary was free, would she like to attend school in New Jersey, to prepare to be a missionary in Liberia? This colony in West Africa had been established for freed people by an American antislavery society.

Many of the other freed slaves continued to live in the Van Lew household, employed by Elizabeth. Mary may have hesitated to leave her friends and relatives, but once she got to school, her quick mind absorbed all the school could teach her. She had a photographic memory, which not only helped with her studies but eventually made her a great spy. Mary worked in Liberia for about five years, returning to Richmond in 1860. Shortly thereafter, she married William Bowser, but the marriage did not last long.

When Confederate President Jefferson Davis moved to Richmond in 1861, he and his wife brought a few of their slaves with them. They needed additional help in the Confederate White House, as they had young children and all manner of social and political obligations.

Mary was soon employed by the Confederate First Lady, perhaps through the recommendation of a friend of Elizabeth's who supplied goods to the Davis household. Elizabeth's spy ring then had the chance to discover what Jefferson Davis himself was hearing. Plans were often lying on his desk or on the side table in the dining room, since no one expected the slaves to be able to read them. One way Mary passed the information along was to the baker Thomas McNiven, another Union spy, when he made deliveries to the house. He was amazed by Mary's memory. She repeated word for word what she'd read.

Mary also met with Elizabeth. She'd set out in the evening, walking quickly, glancing over her shoulder to see who might be following her.

They had time for only hurried conversations, but at least Mary was able to hear how the war was going from the Union's point of view.

When two of the Davis family slaves ran away,[2] Mary was glad they would find freedom. She knew what it was to be free, but even if they had asked her to join them, she wouldn't have gone. She stayed in Richmond until the war was over, playing her part in Elizabeth's spy ring to bring freedom to all slaves.

After the war ended, Mary taught in Georgia at a school for freed people and married a man named Garvin. The date and place of her death is not known.

In 1995, over one hundred years after Mary's secret service ended, the US Army inducted her into the US Army Military Intelligence Corps Hall of Fame for her success "in a highly dangerous mission. She was one of the highest placed and most productive espionage agents of the Civil War."[3]

Mary Surratt's boardinghouse on H Street in Washington, DC, not far from the White House and Ford's Theatre, was a hub of Confederate activity. Her son John carried messages and money to and from Confederate sympathizers throughout the area. John and others whom John Wilkes Booth had recruited met secretly in the boardinghouse. For months in early 1865, they made plans to kidnap President Lincoln. Exactly when Booth gave up on that idea and decided instead to assassinate Lincoln, no one is sure.

Mary believed strongly in the cause of the South. She raised three children and worked tirelessly on her husband's farm and in the tavern he later ran in Surrattsville, Maryland. When he was appointed postmaster, she helped sort mail. After his death in 1862, their son John ran the post office and secretly used it to send letters to Confederate sympathizers. The Surratts' tavern became a Confederate safe house. In 1864, Mary leased the Surrattsville tavern to fellow Confederate-sympathizer John Lloyd and opened the boardinghouse in Washington, DC, where other Confederate sympathizers gathered.

On the afternoon of April 14, 1865, Mary visited John Lloyd in Surrattsville, and gave him a message from Booth. He was to have two guns at the ready that night. Hours after her return to H Street, John Wilkes Booth shot President Lincoln at Ford's Theatre.

Mary Surratt was arrested and brought to trial with others from the boardinghouse. Within three months, she was hanged by the government. Within a few years, all kinds of alternate theories about the assassination plot developed. Even today, historians argue for and against Mary Surratt's guilt. There may never be definitive proof. The boardinghouse on H Street has kept its secrets.

BELLE BOYD

La Belle Rebelle
1844–1900

*S*kirts *flying, sunbonnet tied tightly to her head, Belle dashed across the field. All around, bullets whizzed, some ripping through her skirts. The smell of gunpowder seared her nose and eyes. The crossfire between the Union and Confederate troops in Front Royal, Virginia, would surely hit her before she could deliver her message to General Jackson.*

How had a young Southern lady gotten herself in the middle of a Civil War battle?

Born Maria Isabella Boyd, Belle lived with her parents and seven brothers and sisters in Martinsburg, Virginia (now West Virginia). Belle's father owned a general store and managed a tobacco plantation. They lived in a two-story house covered with roses and honeysuckle.

Even as a child, Belle was a rebel. She climbed trees, raced her horse through the woods, and bossed her playmates around. Once she rode her horse into the house to protest her exclusion from an adult party her parents were planning for that night.

At twelve, Belle was sent to Mt. Washington Female College in Baltimore, Maryland, where she studied French, classical literature, and music. When she graduated at seventeen, she was formally presented to Washington, DC, society. Belle enjoyed the many parties and dances. She was vivacious, attractive, and a brilliant talker. She knew how to make other people feel important.

While she was in Washington, DC, the Civil War broke out, and Belle returned to Martinsburg. She was devoted to helping her people and the rebel cause. At first, she rolled bandages and helped raise money to fund the Confederate army—duties typical of girls of that time. But soon, Belle grew bored and dissatisfied with such tame work. She wanted to do more.

Her chance came when the Union army occupied Martinsburg. Using her wit and natural charm, Belle cajoled military information from Union officers. *What harm would it do to chat with a pretty girl?* the officers thought. Plenty. Belle sent her intelligence via messengers to Confederate leaders. Sometimes she hid the messages inside a hollowed-out watch. She even organized a spy ring with her girlfriends to get information. This was the start of Belle's career as a secret agent, and she was only seventeen.

Soon the Confederate intelligence service appointed Belle as a courier to Generals P. G. T. Beauregard and Stonewall Jackson. Belle hid the military nature of her missions by pretending to be a married woman or a lost girl. A ruse like this let her pass easily across enemy lines. Belle learned to use a cipher and often carried coded messages on horseback, using back roads and shortcuts. Her days as a tomboy paid off! Although she was often detained or arrested, Belle was always let go with a reprimand—until the incident in Front Royal, Virginia.

Belle was visiting her aunt in Union-held Front Royal. General Jackson was on his way to recapture the town as part of his drive against Union General Nathaniel Banks. Belle learned that the Union soldiers planned to blow up the bridges leading from Front Royal as they withdrew, trapping Jackson there. She was determined to warn the general, and taking the message herself seemed the only way.

Belle survived her hair-raising dash across the field. She told one of General Jackson's staff officers all she had learned about the strength and location of Union troops in the Front Royal area. Jackson saved the bridges, which the Union had planned to blow up, and swept northward, nearly to Washington, DC. Belle received a thank-you note from the general himself:

Miss Belle Boyd,

I thank you, for myself and for the Army, for the immense service that you have rendered your country today.

Hastily, I am your friend,

T. J. Jackson, C.S.A.[1]

Belle cherished the letter for the rest of her life.

Already famous in the South, Belle Boyd became notorious throughout the Northern states for the Front Royal incident. She became a celebrity in Europe, too, where the French called her La Belle Rebelle. Belle now was considered dangerous and was imprisoned twice.

Still, she agreed to do one last mission—carry important papers to England to win their help for the Confederate forces. One dark night, using the alias "Mrs. Lewis," she sailed from North Carolina aboard the *Greyhound*, a blockade-runner flying the British flag. Union ships were waiting, and before dawn, the *Greyhound* was seized and a Union crew put on board.

Samuel Hardinge, a young naval officer who commanded the Union boarding party, was in charge of bringing the captured *Greyhound* to New York. On the journey, he fell head-over-heels in love with Belle and proposed marriage. Belle accepted.

But Hardinge allowed the ship's Confederate captain to escape, so he was court-martialed. Belle was taken into custody in New York and banished to Canada under threat of death should she return. From Canada, she sailed to England. After his court-martial hearing, Hardinge was released from the navy, and he, too, went to England where they were married in August of 1864.

Sam returned to the United States, intending to change sides and join the Confederate Army, but he was caught and imprisoned, leaving Belle little money to support herself and their young daughter. Still in England, Belle sold her jewelry and wedding gifts to make ends meet. She also wrote a best-selling memoir. Sam died shortly after he got out of prison, making Belle a widow at twenty-one. Ever resourceful, Belle turned to acting, dramatizing her deeds as a Confederate spy.

In 1865, President Andrew Johnson signed his Proclamation of Amnesty. Belle returned to the United States and continued her stage career. She was invited to speak all around the country. In her lectures, Belle stressed the importance of being a unified country, telling audiences she never thought of herself as a spy, but rather as simply wanting to help her people. This won her support among survivors of both the Union and the Confederacy. In fact, when she died, four Union veterans lowered her coffin into the grave.

PAULINE CUSHMAN

Her Best Role
1833–1893

The theater was packed for the night's performance. Word had passed through the Confederate sympathizers all afternoon—something unexpected was about to happen on stage.

Everyone in the audience leaned forward as Pauline walked out in her role as a fashionable gentleman. She lifted a wine glass as if to drink with a friend. Then she stepped forward and surveyed the audience. Her clear voice rang out: "Here's to Jeff Davis and the Southern Confederacy. May the South always maintain her honor and her rights!"

A shocked silence greeted her, followed by a clatter of both praise and condemnation. The stage manager rushed over. Fellow actors stared in disdain. Pauline wished she could tell them the truth. She really supported the Union, but she made her decision and wouldn't go back on it, even when Union guards arrived to arrest her.

As expected, the stage manager sent a note to her boardinghouse the next morning that read, You will be unable to continue your present role.[1] *Little did he know the new role she was about to play: Union spy.*

Pauline Cushman's birth name was Harriet Wood. She was born in New Orleans, on June 10, 1833. Shortly after, her father lost his business and they moved to a frontier trading post in Michigan. She grew up a tomboy, alongside her brother. She canoed, hunted, and tracked animals through the woods as well as, or better than, he did.[2]

When East Coast culture spread to Michigan, she heard all about the cafés and theaters of New York. That was the life for her! At age eighteen, she moved to New York and headed straight for the theater district. A dazzling beauty, she had no trouble getting into a variety show, and before long she took the stage name Pauline Cushman and was touring with the show in the Southern states.

Pauline married one of the musicians in the show's orchestra, and they had a son and a daughter who died in childhood. When war broke out, her husband became a musician in the Union army. He died from camp fever, a form of typhoid, and Pauline threw herself into her stage career and moved to Louisville, Kentucky, to take a role in the play *Seven Sisters*.

One afternoon, two Confederate officers made a proposal: If she dared to toast the Confederacy that night, they'd give her three hundred dollars.

Pauline was surprised. She and the actors in the company were Northerners. Kentucky was part of the Union. She knew many residents of Louisville sided with the Confederates, but she didn't want that reputation.

The officers persisted, and to get rid of them, Pauline told them she'd think about it. Then she went straight to Union headquarters. The provost marshal, Colonel Orlando H. Moore, could see how this might benefit the Union cause: If the Confederates thought Pauline was a supporter, she would be in a position to gather information about the civilians who met in secret to attack Colonel Moore's soldiers.

It was not something she'd ever considered. But she knew she was good at acting. And from her childhood years, she knew she could sneak through the countryside undetected.

Colonel Moore promised to be at the theater that night, to protect her if the crowd turned on her. After she was arrested, he helped her develop her new role as a Union spy.

Confederate supporters who witnessed Pauline's performance that night welcomed her into their social lives and into their confidence, which helped her gather information. She would also disguise herself as a backward country boy or a young gentleman to eavesdrop on conversations at the billiard parlors and other places where women weren't allowed. In daring night rides into the countryside, she scouted the whereabouts of Confederate troops in the woodlands surrounding Louisville.

Then came a new opportunity. Pauline was invited to join the New Nashville Theatre, in Tennessee. She met with the head of the Union's secret operations in the area. He didn't want to waste this spy on the stage in Nashville. He wanted her to go right into the enemy camps to discover their strengths and weaknesses. He hoped she could meet the famous Confederate General Braxton Bragg and find out his plans.

Pauline's brother was an officer in the Confederate army. Though an argument had driven them apart and she hadn't seen him for years, it would be a perfect cover: a young lady searching for her brother. She was warned not to take notes but to keep everything in her head. If she were caught, she could be tried—and hanged—as a spy.

The thought alarmed her, but Pauline wasn't about to give up. She soon found someone willing to smuggle her across enemy lines. She met up with a Confederate captain, who was so enamored with her, he wanted her to join his troops as his assistant. He had a Confederate uniform made for her. Pauline played along so he wouldn't be suspicious. Though she had no intention of doing so, she promised she'd return to serve with him after she found her brother.

At the next camp she made a big mistake. Pauline had stolen papers from a Confederate officer and hidden them in her shoe. When she finally met up with General Bragg, his detectives found those hidden papers. She tried to act her way out of it. She pouted. She wheedled. She told him she was just a Southern lady who was desperately trying to find her brother.

Listening to her, General Bragg almost felt he could believe her, but the evidence was just too great: the papers in her shoe, the Confederate uniform—a perfect disguise for a Northern spy. General Bragg also questioned why she hadn't smuggled in medicine, such as quinine to prevent malaria, and food, as other Southern ladies were doing.

The general locked Pauline in a room at a nearby inn to await trial. During her trial, Pauline made friends with one of the guards. After days of waiting, she heard the verdict: She was found guilty and would be hanged. Pauline was already physically ill from worry and a feeling of abandonment. Still she didn't have any regret. She did not renounce her country, nor did she betray her mission.

Just when she thought it was all over for her, Pauline was saved. The Union army broke through the enemy lines, forcing General Bragg and his troops to retreat. They left Pauline behind.

She wrapped herself in a blanket and watched the Union troops be welcomed into the city. She recovered from her illness, but she could spy no more. Everyone in the area now recognized her.

At some point, she appropriated the title of major, calling herself Miss Major Pauline Cushman. Beginning in 1864, she toured the country in a military costume, recounting her daring adventures.

As the years passed, interest in the war and Pauline's exploits faded. She remarried in 1872, but her husband died a year later. For several years she worked in logging camps, and then remarried a third time. When she and her third husband, Jeremiah Fryer, separated, she settled in San Francisco. Perhaps nightmares from the close calls she'd had haunted her. The pain from her illness led her to drug dependency, and she died from an apparent accidental overdose.

She was remembered in death, and Civil War veterans and the Women's Relief Corps conducted her funeral. Her simple gravestone, in Officer's Circle at the National Cemetery in the Presidio in San Francisco, reads, *Pauline C. Fryer, Union Spy.*

SARAH EMMA EDMONDS

aka Frank
Thompson
1841–1898

*F*rank felt nervous about being interviewed by three generals, but not about the questions they would ask or the tests he'd have to take. Frank was worried that he'd be found out.

The generals fired questions at him about his loyalty, political views, and willingness to do dangerous work. They tested his ability to handle firearms. They even did a phrenological exam, in which they examined the shape of his skull, because they thought the form of the skull was an indication of character and abilities. When the generals were done, they agreed that Frank Thompson had all of the qualifications to succeed as an undercover agent for the Union's Secret Service.

Except Frank Thompson was really Sarah Emma Edmonds.

Born in New Brunswick, Canada, Emma lived on a farm where she worked very hard. Her father was mean and very strict. Her brother was often sick, so many of the farm chores fell to Emma and her sisters. They dug and sacked potatoes, chopped wood, and tended to the animals. Emma wore pants and heavy shoes. She was strong and lean.

Perhaps because of her harsh life, Emma grew up with an independent spirit and a vivid imagination. Her mother worried about the risks Emma took: She rode the wildest horse, hunted with her father's shotgun, and climbed anything taller than she was. When Emma was twelve, a peddler gave her a novel—the first she'd ever read. It was called *Fanny Campbell, the Female Pirate Captain: A Tale of the Revolution.* The book told of a British girl who disguised herself as a sailor to rescue her sweetheart from pirates. In the book, Fanny rode tough horses, shot panthers, and even cut off her hair for her sailor disguise. It's no surprise that Emma loved reading about Fanny.

When Emma turned fifteen, her father ordered her to marry a man she didn't even know. Emma knew she had to leave. She fled to a nearby city where she learned to make and sell hats. She was only seventeen when she opened her own hat shop.

But the shop wasn't far enough away from her domineering father, who still wanted her to come home. Perhaps inspired by Fanny Campbell, Emma decided to dress as a man and start a whole new life. She lopped off her hair and put on men's clothing. She chose a new name: Frank Thompson. Because of her height, five feet six inches and her dark skin and deep voice, she had no trouble with her disguise. Emma found a job selling Bibles, first in Canada, then in the United States. When the Civil War broke out, she was living in Flint, Michigan.

Personal freedom was very important to Emma. She was against slavery and, though Canadian, she felt deeply loyal to the Union cause. When the Union recruiters came through Flint, Emma decided she wanted to join. Back then, the medical exam to enter the army was simple—just a quick check of the legs and arms to make sure they worked—but Emma failed because she wasn't tall enough. The recruits marched off without her. Later, a Union officer returned to find more recruits. This time, he wasn't so picky.

Farm life had made Emma strong, and she fared as well as the men in basic training. Unlike the city recruits, she felt right at home handling firearms. She was ready to fight alongside the men—and they believed she was a man.

With her regiment, the Second Michigan Infantry, Emma set up camp in Washington, DC, in June 1861. Like the other soldiers, she fired weapons, drilled, stood guard, and marched. For a farm girl, eating the camp hardtack and chewy rabbit soup was no problem at all.

Many men grew sick and died from diseases like typhoid and dysentery without ever reaching a battlefield. In addition to her army duties, Emma volunteered to work in the brigade hospital as a nurse.

That July, the Union's loss at the first battle of Bull Run left troops in a state of shock. The army reorganized, and Emma became a mail carrier for her regiment's camp in Virginia. Then she was recommended for something a little more exciting. She was called to Washington, DC, and questioned by the generals.

Emma answered their questions, handled firearms accurately, and had the right-shaped skull, continuing to pose successfully as Frank. Now she had a chance to serve the Union cause as a secret agent.

Her first mission as a spy was to penetrate the Confederate lines at Yorktown, Virginia, to learn the layout of the camps and how much ammunition was stored there. How could she sneak in undetected? Emma shaved her head, put on a wig of curly hair, and with a silver nitrate solution, colored her skin black. Disguised as a slave called Ned, she slipped into the Confederate camp where she and the other slaves built fortifications and carried water to the troops. As she passed out water, she lingered among the troops and discovered how many reinforcements had arrived. Later, she sketched the fortification, including where guns were mounted and what kinds they were. She hid the information under the insole of one of her shoes. When she carried water to soldiers guarding the outer lines, she stole away to her own camp.

Emma penetrated enemy lines many times in various disguises. On one mission, she was an old Irish peddler. On another, a Confederate guard. Each time she was able to obtain important information for Union forces. Because of her expert riding skills and courage, she was also in constant demand as a courier, carrying messages in the midst of gunfire.

In the spring of 1863, Emma came down with malaria, and afraid of being exposed as a woman if placed in a hospital, she deserted her regiment. She made her way to Ohio, where she recuperated. She began wearing women's clothes again and wrote a book about her war experiences titled *Nurse and Spy in the Union Army: Comprising the Adventures and Experiences of a Woman in Hospitals, Camps, and Battlefields.* It was an instant bestseller.

Still dedicated to the Union cause, Emma returned to nursing, serving in Union hospitals until the close of the war. In Harper's Ferry, West Virginia, she met Linus H. Seelye, a carpenter. They married and had three children, all of whom died young, but they later adopted two sons who survived. Emma and Linus moved frequently, spending much of their time working in orphanages and helping former slaves find jobs and education.

Emma wanted to apply to the government for a veteran's pension, but she knew she'd need help. No one would give a deserter a pension. She decided to call on her former comrades to testify to her loyalty and worth as a soldier. But first she had to tell the truth. She attended a reunion of her regiment, and there she revealed herself as a woman to the men with whom she had served. Instead of being angry at her deceit, they welcomed her as one of their own and, seeing that she was in poor health, gave her their support so that she could gain her pension. It worked, and in July 1884 a special act of Congress acknowledged Emma's service as Franklin Thompson and placed her on the pension roll. They also deleted the charge of desertion from her record.

Emma lived the rest of her life in Texas. In Houston, she was accepted into the Grand Army of the Republic, the premier organization of Civil War veterans. She was the only woman ever to receive this honor. In her memoir, Emma explained that she loved adventure and was ambitious as well as romantic. But patriotism, she said, was the true secret of her success.

Change Your Appearance

With a few tricks of the trade, you can change your appearance the way secret agents do.

- Try using makeup that doesn't match your skin tone, false eyelashes, rouge and lipstick, a fake beauty spot.

- Wear glasses, wigs, and hats from a thrift store.

- Pad your shoulders with rolled-up towels.

- Stuff a wad of gum in each cheek.

- Stick a pebble in one shoe to make yourself limp.

Experiment with different looks. Try to be older, younger, taller, or the opposite sex, like the spies Pauline Cushman and Sarah Emma Edmonds did. Call a friend and set up a meeting spot. See if he calls your name as you walk past. No? Success!

World War I

(1914–1919)

When Archduke Ferdinand of Austria-Hungary was assassinated, reactions from European countries escalated into a full-scale war between two alliances. The Central Powers of Germany, Austria-Hungary, and Turkey fought against the Allies of France, Britain, Russia, and later, the United States.

New technology offered new weapons: planes, tanks, barbed wire. New technology for spying became available, too. Instead of balloons, airplanes did aerial reconnaissance. Telegraph and radio became important tools to send coded messages, and along with those came cryptography, the science of breaking codes.

The United States didn't enter the war until 1917. Women replaced men in offices and factories at home, and it was the first time American women were recruited into military service. They worked as nurses and physical and occupational therapists, as well as operators in the Signal Corps.

Thousands of women in Europe and Britain spied for both sides. Besides operating as couriers, these women ran spy networks and worked as double agents. Spying had become extremely dangerous. The chivalry often shown to women in previous wars was no longer apparent. Women spies who were caught were usually imprisoned. Many were executed.

LOUISE DE BETTIGNIES

Spymaster
1880–1918

---

*T*he German police matron told Louise to take off her clothing. *The gruff woman rubbed Louise's skin with chemicals, hoping to develop a message if something had been penned on her skin in invisible ink. Under Louise's tongue, written on a pellet of rice paper, was a report of German activities. The policewoman was very thorough, and Louise knew she'd eventually find the pellet. Louise quickly gulped it down.*

"What did you swallow?" the woman asked Louise.

"It was nothing," Louise replied. "I'm just tired and a little nervous."

The woman didn't believe Louise and gave her a glass of milk— to calm her nerves, she explained. Louise knew the milk contained something that would make her vomit the message, so she pretended to choke. She dropped the glass, which shattered on the floor. The officer was furious but knew it was too late for another glass—the rice paper was already being digested.

Once again, Louise had narrowly escaped the German Secret Service.

Louise Marie Henriette de Bettignies was born in 1880 in Lille, Belgium, the daughter of a wealthy porcelain manufacturer. She was the seventh of eight children, and her upbringing was typical of many upper-class families at that time: quiet, refined, and uneventful. But Louise was not content to live a dull life. Early on, she showed signs of being exceptionally bright and insisted on going to Oxford University in England, where she studied English, Latin, and literature. She learned to speak several languages.

In the early 1900s, there were few opportunities for young women with a college education, so Louise spent the next ten years as a governess for wealthy families in Austria and Italy. She was educated, fun, and athletic—a perfect governess.

Spy Files

A message written on a shaved scalp would be hidden when the hair grew out.

By her early thirties, Louise had tired of her worldly lifestyle. She wanted to help people and became a Red Cross nurse. When World War I broke out, the Germans swept into Belgium and occupied Lille. Before long, the beautiful city was in shambles. Hospitals and homes were filled with sick and maimed soldiers. Louise was horrified at the brutality of the war and knew she had to take a more active role in stopping it. So she exchanged her Red Cross uniform for plain clothes and began to wander the countryside, memorizing anything about the German's invasion that might help the Allied forces.

To convey her information to the Allies, Louise boarded a ferry for England, posing as a refugee. She astounded British intelligence with all she had discovered and was immediately recruited into the British Secret Service. There, Louise learned about secret inks, codes, and unusual hiding places for messages. Under the secret identity of Alice Dubois, a lacemaker, Louise returned to Belgium to organize a network of spies in the areas that were occupied by the Germans.

Louise immediately gathered together a special group of people. Members included Dr. de Geyter, a chemist who mixed secret inks and forged identity cards, and Paul Bernard, a mapmaker, who could write sixteen hundred words in a space the size of a postage stamp. An old friend, Marie Leonie van Houtte, became Louise's chief assistant. With these few people, the Alice Service was born. Louise's spy network eventually grew to twelve people, then to over twenty. The members rescued and smuggled Allied prisoners of war out of German-occupied territory. They continuously passed military intelligence of vital importance to Louise. It produced the highest-quality information of any network in France or Belgium.

Louise sent messages in ingenious ways. She devised a code of signals using bells. She also converted balls of wool, toys, bars of chocolate, and artificial limbs into hiding places for coded messages. Once she sent the British Secret Service a tiny map hidden in the frame of a pair of eyeglasses that detailed the location of fourteen German ammunition dumps. On another occasion, she handed a German sergeant her identity card so he could stamp the photo. Little did he know that the shiny surface was a layer of thin transparent paper on which Paul Bernard had written a three-thousand-word report in secret ink. Coffins offered a creepy, but effective, way of transporting plans and blueprints: Papers were tightly rolled into a glass tube and inserted into a corpse's windpipe.

Madame Elsie-Julie Leveugle, one of Louise's best agents, lived in a chateau that overlooked Lille's railroad yards. All day and into the night, she would sit by a second-floor window and knit, counting the German railroad cars and troop carriers that rolled by. For each car that passed, Madame Leveugle would tap her foot on the floor. Her son, sitting in the room below, would keep count of the taps and take the tally to Louise.

German counterintelligence officers knew a major spy ring was operating among them and relentlessly searched for the members. But for more than a year, Louise and her agents worked undetected.

Eventually, Louise and Marie Leonie were caught. They were tried

Spy Files

A secret compartment in a glass eye could hold a message on microfilm. The message could escape detection even with a full-body search.

79

by a German military court and sentenced to death. On the day they were to die, their sentences were commuted to twenty-seven years for Louise and fifteen for Marie Leonie.

Because of poor living conditions in prison, Louise grew very sick. Just forty-five days before she would have been freed because of the end of the war, Louise died in prison.

After her death, Louise was awarded the Croix de Guerre and the Ordre de L'Armes for her bravery and service to the Allied forces. In November 1927, a statue of Louise was erected in a small square in Lille, Belgium. Her mother and Marie Leonie were honored guests.

Invisible Ink

For hundreds of years, invisible ink has been an important part of a spy's toolbox. Spies often write their secret messages between the lines of a letter. There are many recipes for invisible ink. Using this one, write a secret message to a friend.

To create your own invisible ink, you'll need:

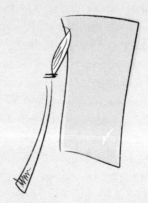

- 1 tsp. baking soda
- 1 tsp. water
- Small cups
- Toothpicks or cotton swabs
- White paper
- Purple grape juice
- Paintbrush

Follow these steps:

1. Mix the baking soda and the water in a small cup.
2. Dip a toothpick or cotton swab into the solution and write a message on white paper. You may need to dip the toothpick often (after writing one or two letters).
3. Let your message dry completely (at least forty-five minutes). You can use a blow dryer to shorten the drying time. Gently wipe off any excess baking soda.
4. Have a friend paint lightly over the area of your message with the grape juice. Voila! Your message will be revealed.

Spotlight:
MABEL ELLIOTT'S DISCOVERY

M abel Elliott became suspicious of a letter written by Anton Kuepferle, a supposed American businessman who had arrived in Liverpool from New York. She worked as a letter censor for the British War Office during World War I and decided to investigate.

Using her simple knowledge of chemistry, Mabel very carefully applied heat to the letter, causing additional words to appear. The words, written in lemon juice, provided details about military forces defending London. Thus began the unraveling of a German spy network that may have aimed to invade Britain. Mabel caught two more spies, accomplices of Anton's.

After the war, Mabel worked for the Royal Society of Chemistry until she retired in 1937, becoming the only woman so far to receive an honorary membership in this organization.

Mabel's role in breaking the German spy network was never acknowledged in her lifetime, because her evidence was given under the assumed name of Maud Phillips. Her contribution was only recently uncovered when the Royal Society of Chemistry was going through its archives and found details of her exploits. In November 2011, the society recognized her on Remembrance Day.

A favorite quote of Mabel's, from novelist Hugh Walpole was: "It isn't life that matters! It's the courage we bring to it."

MARTHE RICHER

Double Agent
1889–1982

*O*il sprayed Marthe's goggles. The flimsy biplane lurched and dipped, but Marthe was determined to land. She banked to the left, into the wind, and headed toward the field.

The ground came up fast. Fifty feet. Twenty feet. Down she went, pulling back on the yoke to hold the aircraft up as long as possible. The wheels thumped the ground, and Marthe's plane rolled to a stop. She climbed out and bowed elegantly to her audience as they clapped and shouted, "Trés bon, Marthe!" Very Good!

At the time of this flight, Marthe was barely out of her teens. Soon the daring and determination she showed flying would be put to the test while spying for her country.

People called her L'Alouette (Lark), but her real name was Marthe Betenfeld. Marthe was born in the eastern part of France in 1889. She learned to fly as a girl, and became one of France's first female pilots. Her sense of adventure didn't stop her from studying hard. She was especially good at languages. Besides her native French, she knew English, German, and Spanish.

After her schooling, Marthe became a dressmaker and opened her own chic shop in Paris. Her feathered hats and lace parasols were a favorite with the French ladies.

In 1914, the year World War I began, Marthe married Henri Richer, a lawyer who had become a pilot for the French military. Just a year later, Henri was killed in action. Marthe was devastated.

Through Henri, Marthe had met Captain Georges Ladoux of the French Counterintelligence Service's Fifth Bureau. Ladoux saw in Marthe the makings of a good spy. She was attractive, cultured, and fluent in several languages. Anxious to avenge her husband's death, Marthe was a willing recruit.

In just a few weeks, Marthe was ready for her first assignment. Posing as a fun-loving Parisian tired of the war, Marthe traveled to Spain to penetrate the German Secret Service. In San Sebastián, which was Spain's main resort city, she took on the role of just another wealthy, glamorous woman looking for a good time. She became well-known in the German social circles and quickly caught the attention of Baron Hans von Krohn, a captain in the German Imperial Navy and the naval attaché to the embassy at Madrid. Von Krohn was old enough to be Marthe's father, but he was smitten with her. When he learned of her cynical attitude toward the war, he knew he could make her a German spy—and, perhaps, his mistress.

Marthe was well aware that as a spy she might have to make difficult and dangerous choices to obtain the results she needed. If she became close to von Krohn, she would be privy to valuable information. She would also be putting her life on the line. But Marthe was passionate about helping the French cause. She agreed to be his mistress.

Spy Files

Hidden cameras were used as early as the 1880s, when they were cleverly placed into hats.

The Germans desperately needed agents in France, and Marthe was quickly put on the payroll of the German Secret Service. Her life as a double agent began.

On one of her first missions, Marthe was sent back to France to find out how many weapons and what types were being produced at a large factory outside of Paris. She left armed with the latest in invisible inks, contained in tiny tablets hidden in her fingernails. She was to use the ink to write her accounts for the German Secret Service. In Paris she made a full report to the Fifth Bureau, which was fascinated with the ink tablets. Until then the French had been able to intercept many messages in the secret writing but unable to develop them. Now that they had the tablets, their chemists could figure out exactly what chemicals were used.

A couple of weeks later, Marthe returned to von Krohn full of "secret" information concocted for her by the experts of the Fifth Bureau. Von Krohn and his chiefs in Berlin were more than satisfied. Von Krohn then sent Marthe to South America with highly secret instructions and supplies for German agents in Brazil and Argentina. These instructions were written in invisible ink on what appeared to be unused notepaper. Marthe was able to help the Fifth Bureau place one of their experts onboard the ship. During the voyage to Buenos Aires, he read the instructions at his leisure.

On another mission, Marthe discovered the secret route through the Pyrenees Mountains used by German agents who infiltrated into France.

Although the Germans paid her for spying for them, Marthe never touched the money. She gave it all to France.

Baron von Krohn had fallen in love with Marthe, but for her, the arrangement was business, and her business was to get intelligence for the French. Von Krohn took her more and more into his confidence, and Marthe's information, often written in the Germany's own secret ink, poured into France.

Spy Files

Moles are enemy agents who penetrate the security services of another agency. They make their way deep into the organization and work invisibly.

When the war came to a close, Marthe returned to France. Before she left, she confessed her role as a double agent to von Krohn. Though shocked, he did nothing about it. He only watched Marthe go.

The Fifth Bureau wanted to honor her service to France, but this suggestion was turned down by authorities who could not stomach the fact that she had been von Krohn's mistress. Marthe was disgusted at their hypocritical attitude and left for England, where she married Thomas Crompton, director of the Rockefeller Foundation. No matter what the French thought, she knew that she had served her country faithfully and well. She did what she thought was best, and the information she had gathered was used to save countless lives. The French government finally agreed, and in 1933 they made her an officer of the Legion of Honor, an honor that Napoleon Bonaparte had established to recognize distinguished service to France.

After Thomas died a few years later, Marthe traveled back to France. During World War II, she came out of retirement. Though well into her fifties, she worked undercover again, this time with the French Resistance.

Spy Files

Double agents don't serve both sides. They deceive one side into believing they are working for it when they are actually stealing its secrets.

86

Spotlight:
MATA HARI'S MISSTEPS

Mata Hari was the stage name for the entertainer Margaretha Geertruida Zelle, born in Holland in 1876. She was an imaginative child who was always pretending. On her sixth birthday, her doting father gave her a child-sized carriage pulled by two tall goats, and he lavished other gifts on her. It was a blow when he lost his business, and he left her with her mother, who soon died. Margaretha went from relative to relative, who mostly felt her spoiled and hard to get along with.

After a miserable failed marriage, Margaretha moved to Paris in her twenties. At first she had trouble finding work, but at parties made up stories about learning sacred dances in the Indies, and Mata Hari was born. She danced throughout Europe and was in Berlin when the Germans entered World War I. Because Mata Hari had gentlemen friends in many countries, she was soon being watched by secret-service organizations on both sides.

Finally, Mata Hari's pretending got her into trouble. She was asked to spy for France, and she got carried away with the idea. She said she wanted one big job and she wanted to be paid one million francs.

Mata Hari was sent to Spain to meet up with a German diplomat. She spent time coaxing information from him, telling him some gossip about French troops to show him she was on the German side. But he caught on to her "spying" and gave her false information. He sent his spies a message that he knew the French would intercept, using an old code he knew they had broken. He implied Mata Hari was spying for the Germans.

Instead of being paid for revealing German secrets when she returned to Paris, Mata Hari was arrested, tried, and executed. Despite her muddled attempt to be a spy, she faced the firing squad with gracious courage.

Spycraft: Spot the Spy

Women spies play an important role in the history of the world, but they also play an important role in books, television, and movies. Can you identify these fictional spies and sleuths? Match the character in the left-hand column to her traits in the right-hand column.

1. Emma Peel	A. 1970s Los Angeles private investigator who, with friends Jill and Kelly, works for Charlie as one of his Angels
2. Harriet M. Welsch	B. 16-year-old computer hacker who joins The Specialists instead of going to juvenile detention; code name GiGi
3. Nancy Drew	C. Student at the seemingly normal Gallagher Academy for Exceptional Young Women in London; code name The Chameleon
4. Sammy Keyes	D. Sensational spylet, aka. Janey Brown; uses lots of spy gadgets including the transformation machine Wower
5. Jane Blonde	E. Martial-arts expert, has reverse-jointed shoulders, knows thirteen languages, works for CIA to dismantle SD-6
6. Sydney Bristow	F. Has a peregrine falcon, carries a red bucket full of seemingly irrational and unnecessary objects; one of the Mysterious Benedict Society
7. Kate Wetherall	G. 1960s Avenger, expert in chemistry and fencing, drives a Lotus Elan, wears black-and-white op art clothes
8. Cammie Morgan	H. Lives with Grams in California, plays softball, has rich best friend Marissa, solves neighborhood mysteries
9. Sabrina Duncan	I. Drives a blue convertible in the 1930s version; now as the "All-New Girl Detective," drives a hybrid
10. Kelly James	J. Lives in New York City, is an aspiring writer, best friends with Sport and Janie, fights the Spy Catcher Club

Answers: 1-G, 2-J, 3-I, 4-H, 5-D, 6-E, 7-F, 8-C, 9-A, 10-B

MARGUERITE HARRISON

Nerves of Steel
1879–1967

B *erlin was still in a state of war, but Marguerite didn't think she'd have any problems reaching her hotel. She got in the cab and waved her travel permit at the driver, who reluctantly started off. As they neared the Hotel Bristol, they heard gunfire. Bullets bounced off the pavement around the car and ricocheted off buildings.*
   "We'd better turn back," said the driver.
   "No, continue on," replied Marguerite sternly. But she wondered if she'd make it through the next few blocks.

Marguerite Elton Baker was born in Maryland in October 1879 to wealthy parents. Her father prospered in Baltimore's shipping trade, and his business grew into the prestigious Atlantic Transport Lines.
   Marguerite and her sister grew up on a beautiful estate near Baltimore. They were raised like royalty, with governesses, nurses, exquisite imported clothes, and trips to England and Europe. Their mother constantly worried about Marguerite's health. Thinking Marguerite was too delicate, she wouldn't let her play sports or have friends over. Far

from her mother's opinion of her, Marguerite was a bold, adventurous young girl. She also loved to read and learned languages easily.

When she was twelve, Marguerite went to live with her grandfather outside Baltimore and attended a nearby private school for girls. Her grandfather was an independent thinker. Marguerite spent a lot of time in his library, which was full of books on travel, exploration, and history. Her grandfather's views helped shape Marguerite's individualism.

Marguerite's mother planned for Marguerite to marry into a well-known, wealthy family, but Marguerite had other ideas. After just one semester at Radcliffe College in Cambridge, Massachusetts, she became engaged to the handsome, but poor, Thomas Bullitt Harrison. Her parents took Marguerite on a European vacation to encourage her to forget Thomas. But it was no use. Headstrong, determined, and in love, Marguerite married him. Nine months later, she gave birth to a baby boy, Tommy, and settled into homemaking. Marguerite and Thomas were happy for fourteen years, but then Thomas died, leaving Marguerite and Tommy penniless.

To support her son, Marguerite turned her Baltimore home into a boardinghouse. This still wasn't enough to make ends meet, so she found a job as an assistant society editor at the *Baltimore Sun* newspaper. When the United States entered World War I, Marguerite covered women's roles in the war effort. To find stories, she drove a streetcar and worked as a laborer at Bethlehem Steel. Her expert language skills opened doors to interviews other reporters could not handle.

Marguerite wanted to do more for the war cause than just report from the home front. She was especially curious about what life was like in Germany, a country she had visited in peacetime with her family. Europe was one vast battlefield, with Germany in the center of it. Entering Germany was nearly impossible. But not for Marguerite! She knew one way to get in: She'd become a spy.

She applied to the chief of the army's Military Intelligence Division (MID), General Marlborough Churchill. Marguerite impressed the general with her good looks, confidence, and fluency in so many languages. But as she was about to leave for Europe, the war ended. Marguerite thought her career as a spy was over before it even started; however, MID had a new assignment for her. She was to go to Europe to report social, economic, and political matters to the US delegation at the forthcoming peace conference. Marguerite was given a code name and cipher tables. She would travel as a newspaper correspondent on special assignment to the *Baltimore Sun* and write feature articles for the paper while collecting intelligence on the social and economic condition of Germany.

Marguerite's goal was to get to Berlin, the capital of Germany. Europe was in chaos. Roads were in ruins, and trains were packed with people trying to return to their homes. It took weeks of hitchhiking on army transports for Marguerite to reach Germany. Not all of the country was occupied by the Allies yet, and conflicts raged between groups of Germans who disagreed on who should govern the country. Fighting continued in many areas, including the streets of Berlin around the Hotel Bristol.

With bullets still whizzing, Marguerite and the cabbie pulled up in front of the hotel. Every curtain was pulled, every shutter was closed, and the heavy wrought-iron doors were bolted tight. The driver dumped her bags onto the sidewalk and took off without saying a word. She rang the bell and waited, pressed as closely as possible against the door. A night porter cracked the door open and poked his head out. When he saw Marguerite, he grabbed her bags and yanked her inside.

This was the start of Marguerite Harrison's life as a foreign correspondent and spy.

Marguerite quickly found her way around Berlin, mingling with people of high and low society, trying to make contact with every sort of political party. She could not overlook any happening, great or small, that might throw light on conditions in Germany. In the dead of night, after a theater performance or dinner party, Marguerite would write long reports for MID. To keep her cover, she also filed stories for the *Baltimore Sun*.

Life as a spy was hard. For hours and hours Marguerite followed rumors and leads. She was always worried about being discovered. She had heard what happened to wartime spies like Mata Hari. There was nothing glamorous about her job!

The signing of the Versailles peace treaty in June 1919 ended Marguerite's intelligence work in Berlin. Back in Baltimore, she realized that working for the *Sun* would not satisfy her appetite for being part of the international scene. So she turned her attention toward Russia, which was in the middle of the Communist Revolution.

The Communists had overthrown the Russian elite. The country was in turmoil. Marguerite was curious about conditions there and proposed to MID to let her operate in Moscow as she had in Berlin.

It was very dangerous to enter Russia as a secret agent. Violence, terror, and executions were commonplace. Marguerite didn't speak Russian. She had no visa and would have to enter secretly by whatever route she could. Her assignment was brief: Get into Russia, sum up conditions in Moscow and other key cities, and return in a few months.

With her son Tommy at school in Switzerland, and a companion to interpret for her, Marguerite set out for the Polish-Russian border. In the winter of 1920, she dashed across the border, first in a sleigh, then on foot. When she arrived in Moscow, she discovered that newspaper correspondents from the United States were not welcome. Officials said she could stay for only two weeks.

Instantly taken with the Russian people, Marguerite began to collect information as she had in Germany. She attended all kinds of meetings and talked with many types of people. She visited museums and absorbed all she could about Russian artists and writers. She was elated when told she could stay an additional month in Moscow.

One night, when Marguerite was walking back to her apartment from the foreign office where she filed her stories, she was stopped and arrested by a soldier. She was accused of being a spy. The Cheka, the

Spy Files

As early as 100 BC, Julius Caesar used homing pigeons to send messages to his troops. Hundreds of thousands of pigeons carried messages in World War I. Some even carried small cameras to take photographs of the enemy. During World War II, many a downed airman owed his life to a homing pigeon he let go as he bobbed in a tiny raft in the ocean.

secret police, even had a copy of one of her secret messages to MID from Germany. Marguerite was taken to the feared Lubianka prison.

At first she was alone in a dark, tiny cell. Then, after several weeks, she was taken to a small room full of other women. The women had to clean the one toilet that served all of them. They hunted rats for food and made up entertainment to keep away madness. Despite their efforts, some women went crazy and were taken away raving.

Marguerite became ill and was finally moved to a better prison with real beds and flowers in the yard, but she was sure she'd die before she was freed. Back in Baltimore, Marguerite's friends and coworkers from the *Sun* and MID worked to save her. Finally, she was released—still sick and thin, but alive.

Once home, Marguerite recuperated and devoted herself to lecturing and writing about her adventures in Moscow. But soon the luxuries she had dreamed of in prison became boring. So Marguerite headed to Japan to write a series of magazine articles about the Far East. This was the start of more adventures that took Marguerite around the world. Her travels included helping to make a landmark documentary film that followed a branch of the Bakhtiari tribe of Persia (now Iran) as its members and their herds made their seasonal journey to better pastures.

Spy Files

American Indian code talkers from seventeen tribes joined US armed forces in World Wars I and II, the most famous being the Navajo, who worked as Marines in the Pacific in World War II. They used words from their traditional languages for secret battle communications, and America's enemies never deciphered their coded messages.

At age forty-seven, Marguerite married an English actor and settled down. After his death in 1949, she returned to Baltimore to live near her son. She continued to travel and even returned to post–World War II Berlin. When she was in her eighties, she traveled alone through forbidden Communist East Berlin—once again showing her steely nerve and adventurous spirit.

While American women did not operate overseas as spies in World War I, many worked stateside as code breakers, cracking codes and ciphers devised by enemies of the Allies. The War Department came to rely on hundreds of American women who served as cryptographers. Meet these two pioneers in the field, both honorees in the Hall of Fame at the National Cryptologic Museum at Fort Meade, Maryland:

Agnes Meyer Driscoll enlisted in the navy in 1918, just after the United States entered the war. With her impressive background in foreign languages, mathematics, and physics, she was assigned to the Code and Signal Section of the Director of Naval Communications. Agnes helped develop one of the navy's first machines to tackle mathematically based codes. This math whiz also worked on Enigma, the famously complicated machine used by the German military to encode and decode secret messages. When Agnes retired from the navy, she joined the National Security Agency (NSA).

Elizebeth Friedman had a knack not only for learning languages but also for detecting patterns and irregularities in them. This skill landed her a job at Riverbank, a facility in Illinois that studied cryptology. Elizebeth and her husband, cryptologist William F. Friedman, left Riverbank in 1921 to found the War Department's Signals Intelligence Service. In 1923, the US Navy employed her as a cryptanalyst to help thwart international smugglers and drug runners by deciphering their encrypted radio messages. Elizebeth also broke a code used by one of espionage's most famous spies, Velvalee Dickinson, a Japanese agent operating in the United States during World War II.

World War II

(1939–1945)

In World War II, Germany, Italy, and Japan—referred to as the Axis powers—fought against the Allies of Britain, France, the Soviet Union, and the United States. By 1940 most of continental Europe was occupied by Germany and under the control of the Axis powers.

Following Japan's attack on Pearl Harbor in 1941, the United States joined the war, sending troops to Europe and Asia.

Many of the countries had well-established foreign intelligence networks. The British Special Operations Executive (SOE) supported resistance movements and underground organizations that used guerrilla warfare. They also conducted sabotage and intelligence operations in enemy-occupied territory. The United States formed the Office of Strategic Services (OSS) to play a similar role. Together, and with local resistance groups, the SOE and OSS created chaos behind enemy lines in both Europe and Asia.

By World War II, women had become an integral part of the US military, serving not only as nurses, but as pilots, truck drivers, and mechanics. And they spied, with many working undercover in the resistance networks. They put themselves in harm's way to send messages, carry arms and supplies, set up rendezvous, and organize escapes.

VIRGINIA HALL

Wanted! The
Limping Lady
1906–1982

The wanted poster circulated by the Gestapo warned, The woman who limps is one of the most valuable Allied agents in France, and we must find and destroy her.[1]
But that didn't stop Virginia.

Virginia Hall was born in 1906 in Baltimore, Maryland, to a prominent family. She loved sports and drama. She played baseball, hockey, and tennis and acted in plays as early as age eight. Virginia was lucky to have a father who owned several movie theaters, so she and her friends could see the movies for free.

In the summers, Virginia spent time on her family's farm outside of the city. She milked cows and cared for other animals. Little did she know how valuable her farm skills would later become.

Like her grandfather, who had stowed away on a clipper ship, Virginia yearned for a life of adventure. She wanted to travel and live in faraway places. Virginia started college in the United States, but she continued her studies in Paris and Vienna, where she learned to speak French,

German, and Italian. After her studies, Virginia worked as a clerk with the US State Department in Eastern Europe. She thought a career overseas would offer her just the kind of excitement she longed for.

Then tragedy struck. While hunting in Turkey, Virginia's gun discharged by mistake and riddled her left leg with shotgun pellets. To save her life, her leg was amputated. Undaunted, Virginia learned to walk with an artificial leg, which she nicknamed Cuthbert.

After World War II broke out, Virginia left her job. She wanted to play a more active role in fighting the Nazis, so she enlisted in the French army as an ambulance driver and later joined the SOE. The commanding officers were impressed by her courage, energy, self-confidence, and cool judgment, perfect qualities for a special agent. At the SOE, Virginia learned about weapons, communications, and security, all of the information she would need to become a spy.

Virginia's first assignment was to work undercover as a reporter for the *New York Post* while setting up operations in France. Working with the French underground, she helped downed American aircrews and prisoners of war escape from enemy territory. She still found time to write for the *Post* not only to protect her cover but also to tell Americans how difficult life was for the French people as more and more German soldiers poured into the country, taking over homes and businesses.

Eventually it became too dangerous for Virginia, and she too had to leave France. Despite her wooden leg, she hiked in the dead of winter through the Pyrenees Mountains to get to Spain. Her wooden leg became very painful, and in a message to SOE headquarters in London, she wrote, "Cuthbert is giving me trouble, but I can cope." A London agent who didn't know her replied, "If Cuthbert is giving you trouble, have him eliminated."[2]

Even after experiencing the danger in France, Virginia longed for another assignment. Back in England, she trained to be a radio operator. Under the code name Diane, she returned to occupied France, this time working with the US OSS. Her mission: to maintain radio contact with London, put together sabotage plans, and form guerrilla groups to fight the Nazis.

The wanted posters for her were plastered everywhere. To avoid the Gestapo, who had learned about her through French double agents,

Virginia moved often and wore the long, heavy clothes of a peasant to hide her limp. For a while, she stayed on a farm in the French countryside. She milked cows and led them to pasture, noting which fields would make good spots for parachute drops. Later she moved to another house and hid her radio equipment in the attic. There she exchanged cows for a herd of goats. She tended the herd along roads where she could watch German troop movements. Delivering goat milk turned out to be a perfect way to make contact with the local resistance.

Despite the Gestapo's intensive search for her, Virginia continued to send radio messages to London about German army activities. She also organized farmhands to receive parachute drops of weapons and supplies from England. Although her leg kept her from being trained in guerrilla warfare, Virginia became a superb leader. Her resistance teams destroyed bridges, derailed freight trains headed for Germany, downed key telephone lines, and took Nazi prisoners.

The Gestapo never found the Limping Lady.

At the war's end, Virginia received America's Distinguished Service Cross. She was the only female civilian in the war to receive this high honor. Virginia continued to use her skills and experience as one of the first women employed by the Central Intelligence Agency (CIA), the successor organization to the OSS. She went overseas on several more assignments but spent her last years with the CIA in Washington, DC.

Reflecting on her career, Virginia said, "I look to the new achievements the next generation will accomplish as they carry the torch into the future, and I hope that they will follow my example and never let anything hold them back."[3]

Spotlight:
JULIA CHILD'S SHARK REPELLENT

Julia McWilliams was fun loving and mischievous. She was born in 1912 in Pasadena, California. As a child, she played tennis, wrote stories, and performed plays. She loved to take her father's cigars and smoke them in a hiding place with friends.

Julia went to Smith College in Northampton, Massachusetts, where she majored in history. Over six feet tall, Julia was a key player on the basketball team. In college, she kept everyone laughing with her great sense of humor.

When World War II broke out, Julia volunteered with the Red Cross in Pasadena and then got a clerical job in Washington, DC, with the OSS. There she helped develop a shark repellent to keep sharks from bumping into underwater explosives and setting them off. Her recipe for this repellent is still used today.

Julia then volunteered to help staff a new overseas OSS base in Ceylon (now known as Sri Lanka). Important missions against the Japanese were launched from that area, and the OSS provided the US military and State Department with intelligence about the enemy. While in Ceylon, Julia met the worldly, sophisticated Paul Child, who also worked for the OSS. With Paul, she experienced the joy of good food.

They fell in love and married when they returned to the United States. Later, Paul was stationed in Paris with the US State Department, and Julia went with him. While living in Paris, Julia trained as a professional chef. She introduced French cooking to Americans in what would become an iconic cookbook and, later, a television show. After her death in 2004, her entire kitchen was set up in the Smithsonian Institution in Washington, DC.

GERTRUDE SANFORD LEGENDRE

Making Her Mark
1902–2000

A driver in a small car picked up Gertrude and raced through war-torn Frankfurt. There Gertrude boarded a train for Switzerland, shadowed by a tall stranger in a light overcoat.

Once on board, Gertrude kept out of sight, hiding behind empty seats. The train moved slowly, inching along battered tracks. It stopped just short of the gate on the German side of the border. Gertrude wasn't safe yet. She slipped off the train. What should she do next? She turned around to see the mysterious man right behind her.

"Run," he whispered and gestured with his arm toward the Swiss guard post.[1]

Gertrude ran. Suddenly she heard, "Halt!" It was an armed German border guard. She'd been seen.

An independent tomboy from the start, Gertrude Sanford was born in Aiken, South Carolina, in 1902. She was the youngest of three children: her brother, Laddie, was oldest; then came sister Janie; and then Gertie, as she was called as a child.

Gertrude grew up in rural New York State, where her family made carpets and raised thoroughbred horses. When she was a teenager, her family moved to New York City. Gertrude's mother took in the lavish Roaring Twenties lifestyle; there were always parties, dances, musicals, and theater to attend.

But Gertrude wanted more than a whirling social life. At the Foxcroft School in Virginia, she was greatly influenced by the headmistress, who convinced all the girls to make their own mark in life.

Hunting in the country had always been part of her early life and it became a lifelong passion. At age eighteen, instead of staying in New York for the debutante parties, Gertrude hunted in the Grand Tetons. At twenty-five, she went on her first African safari.

In London, during the summer of 1928, she met tall, handsome Sidney Legendre. Sidney accompanied Gertrude to Africa to collect specimens for the American Museum of Natural History in New York. They fell in love and married, settling down in South Carolina on a large plantation called Medway.

When World War II began, Sidney entered the navy. Gertrude wanted to be part of the war effort too, so she volunteered with the OSS in Washington, DC. She worked her way up from file clerk to head of the cable desk, where she monitored communications from US secret agents all over the world. On her desk were piles of folders stamped *Restricted*, *Confidential*, *Secret*, and *Top Secret*. Knowledge of such vital information was an enormous responsibility.

Soon Gertrude transferred to the OSS office in London as chief of the Central Cable Desk. She handled incoming messages for thirteen OSS branches in London. The steel safes in her office were filled with secret files from North Africa, Italy, Sweden, India, China, Ceylon (now Sri Lanka), and outposts in German-occupied France.

Gertrude was then reassigned to an OSS center in Paris. While the offices were being renovated, she obtained a five-day pass—a well-deserved chance to do what she wanted for a few days. Whether it was her sense of adventure or her desire to see action after so many months behind a desk, Gertrude certainly didn't expect her next decision to be such a dangerous one.

Accompanied by OSS colleagues Bob Jennings and Major Max Papurt, Gertrude decided to see what it was like at the battlefront. They created a cover story for Gertrude, since she was a civilian and a woman. With the major's driver, they set out in a jeep for Wallendorf, a small German village near the front lines. Just as they neared the signpost for Wallendorf, bullets hit the jeep. The people inside hurled themselves to the ground. But Papurt and the driver were hit, and there was nothing to do but surrender. Jennings pulled a white handkerchief from his pocket and tied it to the end of Papurt's rifle. He hoisted it high above the jeep.

With the Germans nearly upon them, Gertrude quickly burned their passes and any other papers that would link them to the OSS. At the same time, they came up with believable cover stories.

The driver and Papurt were transferred to a medical unit, but Gertrude and Jennings were taken to a bunker and interrogated. Gertrude repeated her cover story in French: She was a clerk at the American Embassy acting as a translator for Jennings. They had been misinformed that Wallendorf was in American hands. She knew nothing of any importance.

Gertrude recited her cover story many times during the next six months. She was moved from prison to prison. At one, housed in a huge castle, Gertrude noticed that Lieutenant William Gosewich, the German officer in charge, spoke fluent English, with just a trace of a New York accent. Gosewich interrogated Gertrude every evening. Over the next several weeks, his questioning became more relaxed. Gertrude learned that he had gone to school in New York City and had married an American. They had lived in the United States for eighteen years. He and his family were visiting Germany when the war broke out, and Gosewich had been forced to serve. He loved his native Germany but opposed the war.

Gertrude formed a friendship with Gosewich that probably saved her life. Gosewich was sorry Gertrude was captured and worked to get her released. He also tried to keep the infamous Gestapo away from her.

One day Gosewich told Gertrude he had been called to the front for three weeks. While he was gone, Gertrude was taken to Gestapo headquarters in Berlin. Despite intense interrogation, Gertrude never revealed anything. Finally, she was transferred to a large estate-turned-prison, where she was able to contact Gosewich. He came to see her and planned her escape to Switzerland.

When Gertrude approached the Swiss border, she didn't stop when she heard the German border guard call, "Halt!" She ran still faster toward the Swiss gate. The German guard's footsteps grew closer.

The Swiss sentry shouted, "*Identite! Identite!*" all the while raising his gate.

"American passport!" Gertrude screamed and passed under the lifted barrier.[2]

Safely in Switzerland, Gertrude was met by OSS officials with hundreds of secrets still safe. She was sent home and reunited with her husband and family. Gertrude never knew why the German guard didn't shoot her. When her husband got out of the navy, they returned to Medway and continued their life of traveling and hunting. Gertrude was able to pay back Lieutenant Gosewich's kindness by helping him and his family return to the United States.

Sidney died of a heart attack in 1948, but Gertrude continued to travel, visiting exotic places such as the Galapagos Islands, New Guinea, and the Amazon. She grew concerned about the plight of endangered animals and turned her plantation into a center for saving endangered birds. At the time of her death in 2000, Medway Plantation became a wildlife preserve.

Spotlight:
HEDY LAMARR'S INVENTION

Before Hedy Lamarr moved from Europe to Hollywood to pursue a career in movies, she was married to Friedrich Mandl, an Austrian arms dealer. While her role at her husband's business meetings was to look beautiful, her brain was always in high gear, absorbing many details about weaponry.

At a party in Hollywood during World War II, Hedy met an avant-garde musician, George Antheil, and they discussed the war in Europe. Hedy had been horrified at the deaths of London schoolchildren whose ship was torpedoed by German U-boats while they were escaping to Canada. She began to think about something that might have prevented this—a radio-controlled torpedo steered from an airplane. George was an expert on making machines work in synchrony—he had once synchronized four player pianos at a concert. With his help, Hedy designed a new kind of torpedo guidance system. The radio transmitter and receiver could hop in synchrony randomly, from frequency to frequency. A constantly changing frequency could not be detected or jammed.

Hedy and George patented their concept in 1942 and offered it to the navy. The navy did not take them or their invention seriously. Their device was never used during the war.

Hedy didn't make a dime on her invention. By the late 1950s, the patent expired, but engineers at Sylvania "rediscovered" it, calling it spread spectrum. It became a basic tool for secure military communications and is the basis for antijamming devices used today, including Milstar, the US government's defense communications satellite system. Cell phones, Bluetooth networks, and GPS devices also rely on Hedy's idea.

Spotlight:
ALICE'S ACE

Alice Marble learned to play tennis on San Francisco's public courts in 1928, when she was fifteen. Her fame as an attractive, vivacious player grew throughout the country. She could serve ace after ace. In 1939, Alice won Wimbledon, becoming the number-one female player in the world.

World War II ended her international competitions. When Alice's pilot husband was shot down over Germany and killed, she agreed to work for US intelligence who suspected her former Swiss lover of holding money, art, and jewels for Nazis at his Swiss bank. Alice's mission was to find his list of Nazis and photograph it. To get ready, she learned defensive tactics and how to shoot guns and crack safes.

Using tennis as a cover, Alice traveled to Geneva in 1945 to play in tournaments. Hans Steinmetz (not his real name) found her and rekindled their relationship, just as she and her handler had hoped. One night Alice sneaked to the basement of Hans's chateau, opened his safe, and found the list of Nazi names. Hans caught her just after she finished photographing the list. She escaped in his car, but she was stopped by a double agent who grabbed the camera and shot her in the back.

When Alice woke up in the hospital, her handler said her dangerous work had been for nothing. But that was far from the truth. Alice possessed a photographic memory, and when she closed her eyes, the Nazis' names reappeared.

Among those later tried at the International Military Tribunal at Nuremberg were men whose names she had remembered from her hospital bed.

Alice had aced her opponent again.

MARIA GULOVICH

Shadow Warrior
1921–2009

The Gestapo started at each end of the train, checking everyone's luggage. The train was so packed that Maria had to stand. She clutched the suitcase she was carrying for members of the Slovak underground, rebels. It was locked, and she had no key. She didn't know what was inside, only that it was important. She couldn't let the Gestapo get their hands on it.

Across from her was a compartment full of German officers on their way to the front. Maria smiled at one of them. She tried to look uncomfortable wedged between the passengers. Luckily, the officer offered Maria a place to sit. He took her suitcase, and she went inside their compartment. Just then, the Gestapo passed by. They saluted the officers and kept going. If they had discovered the radio inside the suitcase, Maria would have been arrested and shot.

Maria Gulovich was born in 1921 in the Slovak village of Jakubany, near the border with Poland. She was the oldest of six girls. Maria's father, Edmund, was a Greek Orthodox priest and her mother, Anastasia, was a teacher. Jakubany was very rustic, with no electricity or running water. There was one telephone at the post office, and the grocery store was several miles away. Most people farmed, logged, or raised sheep for a living. Between school and chores, Maria didn't have much free time. Whenever she could, she hid in the hayloft of the barn and read books. During summer vacations, she went into the nearby hills and gathered strawberries and mushrooms. In the winter, she sewed dresses for her sisters.

Maria started school in a one-room schoolhouse, but her father worried that she wasn't getting a good education. He eventually sent Maria to two different convents in the city of Presov. It was not easy for Maria to conform to the strict convent lifestyle. She was free-spirited and had a mind of her own, but she was also a good student. She studied literature and history. She already knew how to speak Hungarian and Rusyn (a dialect of Russian), and at school she learned to speak Russian, German, and Slovak.

When Maria turned fourteen, her father sent her to Vienna to live with an aunt and begin an apprenticeship as a dressmaker. Maria loved Vienna with its rich culture and museums. There was so much to see and do. Eventually, Maria enrolled in a teacher's college. She began teaching school in a town not far from her family home in Jakubany. Maria enjoyed being a teacher, but with the arrival of the war, the job did not last long.

The new German regime, the Third Reich, occupied most of Czechoslovakia. In Slovakia, where Maria lived, the people were supposedly free, but Hitler's puppet government and local Nazis controlled almost all aspects of their lives. They hunted down anyone who didn't agree with them. Maria hated that her country was under Nazi rule.

Soon after Maria started teaching, her school was taken over by the German army. The Nazis planned to invade the Soviet Union, and the little town of Jarabina where she taught was along the route. They wanted to use the town as a staging area for German armed forces.

In the spring of 1943, Maria moved to the farming community of Hrinova, and for a while she taught school there. Some of the Slovak people organized an underground movement to help the Allies defeat Germany and reclaim their country. Maria decided to join them.

Going undercover as an apprentice dressmaker, Maria moved to the new resistance headquarters in Banska Bystrica and carried secret messages for the Slovak underground. It was a dangerous job, but Maria was dedicated to freeing her people from Nazi control. Maria later worked as a translator and interpreter for the Russians in Banska Bystrica who were organizing guerrilla groups to fight the Nazis. She translated Slovak messages from the front line into Russian.

Now that a strong resistance movement was in place in Slovakia, the OSS flew in agents to help the uprising and rescue downed US airmen. Maria met some of them when they came to Banska Bystrica.

No one expected the Germans to react so strongly to the uprising. Huge numbers of troops poured into Slovakia to break up the rebellion. They bombed the airfield and Banska Bystrica every day. The OSS couldn't get all of the downed airmen out. The Slovak underground was collapsing.

The Germans tightened their net around Banska Bystrica. Nearly everyone left the city, including Maria and the American agents. They headed for Donovaly, a ski resort in the Tatra foothills. But by the time they arrived, the ski resort had to be abandoned because German troops were advancing so quickly. Maria, along with downed Allied pilots, members of the British and American intelligence teams, and other refugees, pushed deeper into the frigid, unmapped trails of the Tatra mountains—the only way to the Russian front and their freedom. They had no idea what lay ahead.

They decided to split into smaller groups. Since Maria knew the area, she helped lead an OSS team of twenty men, acting as their guide and interpreter. They always were just ahead of their Nazi pursuers. Whenever they could, they camped in abandoned huts in the mountains and foraged for food at farms and villages. Food was so scarce that they once had to eat a dead horse to survive. They began to suffer from frostbite. Their feet swelled and turned black.

While looking for food, six people in Maria's group were captured by the Germans. Maria and the rest finally reached the mountain resort village of Velky Bok, where the British had set up refuge in a hotel. Maria and the OSS team spent Christmas Eve in a nearby hut, safe for a few days. On Christmas Day, Maria, two OSS agents, and two British officers headed for the hotel. While they were gone, Nazis surrounded the hut, took everyone captive, and set fire to it.

For twenty-three more days, they marched toward the Russian front, suffering from hunger and cold. Several times they were nearly captured. At the end of January, Maria and her tattered group huddled in an abandoned mine shaft near the village of Bystre, not far from the Hungarian border where the Russians were fighting. They lay like logs, packed tightly, head to toe. After a week, they moved to a larger mine with many other refugees.

One day they heard shouting. The Germans had abandoned Bystre. Allied forces occupied the village. They were free!

It was five more months before Maria finally made it to OSS headquarters in Italy, where she would be truly free. General William Donovan, head of the OSS in Washington, DC, arranged for Maria to go to the United States in January 1946 as an exchange student.

Spy Files

Some World War II spies concealed escape maps in a deck of playing cards; peeling each card apart revealed an area of the map.

On a spring day in 1946, at a ceremony at West Point, General Donovan pinned the Bronze Star onto Maria for her heroic actions. At just twenty-four years old, she became the first woman to be decorated at West Point in front of the Corps of Cadets.

Maria settled down in the United States. She lived in California with her husband, Hans Liu, until her death in 2009.

In 1945 two of the men Maria accompanied to the Russian front wrote: "Her courage and abilities are admired and appreciated by all the men, especially us, whom she accompanied through the lines. She is responsible for our being alive today."[1]

JOSEPHINE BAKER

Forever Grateful

1906–1975

R ap-rap-rap. The knocks were loud and insistent. Josephine hurried the other spies into a back room before opening the door: Five German officers pushed past her, demanding to search her chateau for weapons.

Josephine took command of the situation, just as she always did on stage. Josephine was an African American and she also had some Cherokee ancestry. When they said "weapons," it made her think of tomahawks. She joked that there were no tomahawks in her home. "And," she added, "the only dance I've never taken part in is the war dance." [1]

The officers laughed, chatted with her for a while, and then left without doing a search. Josephine and the other spies hiding in her chateau were safe—for the moment.

Josephine Baker's given name was Freda Josephine, but her family called her Tumpy, because as a baby she was roly-poly like Humpty Dumpty. She was born on June 3, 1906, in St. Louis, Missouri, to

Carrie McDonald. Carrie later married Arthur Martin, and they raised Josephine and her siblings in extreme poverty. One year, Josephine wore the same blue dress to school every day. Students teased her mercilessly.

When Josephine was ten years old, a traveling salesman came through town and set up a dance competition to advertise his wares. Josephine entered, and won. It amazed her that she could earn money doing something she loved.

When Josephine joined the vaudeville circuit, she traveled throughout the eastern United States. She married Willie Baker and settled in Philadelphia. But she kept dancing and acting in clubs until one day she realized if she were to fulfill her dreams, she'd have to move to New York. She went alone.

She joined a chorus line and soon stole the show with her comic antics as well as her amazing dancing. She was invited to join a touring show heading for Paris and, once there, discovered that Paris was the place for her. She didn't experience the same racial prejudice as in the United States. Josephine became a star, performing on stages all over Europe.

When the Nazis came to power in Germany, Josephine's picture appeared on the cover of a propaganda pamphlet denouncing many famous performers who did not meet the Nazi ideals of racial purity. One terrible night in 1938, Nazis attacked Jewish homes throughout Germany and Austria. Josephine, who by then had married a Jewish man, determined to stand up publicly for her beliefs. She joined the International League Against Racism and Anti-Semitism and was soon recruited by French military intelligence.

Josephine was not afraid of possible consequences. "France made me what I am," she said. "I will be grateful forever. . . . [The people of Paris] have given me their hearts, and I have given them mine. I am ready . . . to give them my life."[2]

She began her undercover work at the embassy parties she was often invited to because of her stardom. While laughing and talking with other guests, Josephine listened carefully to talk about German troop strength and locations and passed it on to the French. She was most famous for getting the original copy of the German-Italian codebook.

During this time, Josephine also helped serve meals to refugees who flooded into Paris. As the Germans advanced into France, she visited the injured in hospitals, sometimes cheering them by singing in the wards.

Then Paris was invaded. The show Josephine was starring in closed down. From her chateau in southern France, she continued her work with the French Resistance. As an actress, Josephine was allowed to travel across borders to perform in other countries. Her sheet music often had top-secret information written in invisible ink between the bars of music. Eventually, she went to North Africa and performed throughout the area, raising money for the French Resistance.

After the war, Josephine received many awards from the French government for her war service, including the Croix de Guerre, the Legion of Honor, and the Rosette of the Resistance. She toured the United States several times, taking opportunities to speak out for civil rights. She was on the platform in front of the Lincoln Memorial in Washington, DC, with Martin Luther King, when he gave his famous "I Have a Dream" speech in 1963.

But her home was in France. Josephine never gave up the stage. Following the opening of a new show to celebrate her fiftieth year of performing, she suffered a stroke and died. The people of Paris gave her their hearts once again. They lined the streets as her coffin passed to honor their star, their war hero, and their champion of freedom and equality.

Several years before her death, a committee of distinguished people proposed that Josephine win the Nobel Peace Prize. She told them she didn't deserve it, saying, "It should be shared by each man and each woman on this Earth who struggles to love and live in peace."[3]

Spy Close-up
Josephine's Rainbow Tribe

After the war, Josephine Baker reflected on the horrors she had witnessed. She wondered what it would take for people to work together to prevent other wars.

An idea grew within her. She was by then married to Jo Bouillon, and together they adopted twelve children from differing ethnic and religious backgrounds. The children were raised together, free from prejudice. She called them her Rainbow Tribe and hoped they would be ambassadors of peace in the world.

Josephine continued touring and performing. It took a lot of money to raise twelve children. However, in the United States, she canceled performances in venues that excluded blacks. Stress took a toll on her health. Her marriage broke up, and she lost her family home. She had plans for each of the children, but they rebelled when they hit their teen years. After Josephine's death, the members of the Rainbow Tribe went their separate ways, desiring to live ordinary lives. Many of them are still alive today.

NOOR
INAYAT
KHAN

Light of
Womanhood
1914–1944

S *aturday, June 26, 1943. Madeleine couldn't believe her ears. All the members of the spy team she'd just joined had been arrested— all but her. Her fingers tapped quickly, transmitting the message to* London. It's too dangerous for you now, *the British officials replied.* Come back. Immediately!

But Madeleine knew there was no other wireless operator in her network in Paris. How would secret messages get through without her? She decided to take her chances. She had the courage to stay in earshot of the Gestapo.

Madeleine was the code name for Noor Inayat Khan, one of the Gestapo's most sought-after British spies. Noor's given name, Noor-un-nisa, means Light of Womanhood. She was born on January 1, 1914, in Moscow. Her father, Hazrat Inayat Khan, had been invited to perform there with his musical group. He began to spread the messages of Sufism, an Islamic mystic philosophy that teaches acceptance of all religions, all ideas.

When the Russian Revolution broke out, the family fled to London, England, where three more children were born. The British Home Office grew suspicious of Noor's father during India's independence movement, even though he was a part of a group formed to bring Muslims and non-Muslims together. The family moved to France, settling in Suresnes, a small town on the outskirts of Paris. Both of Noor's parents were deeply spiritual. Her mother, Ora Ray Baker, was American born and a relative of the founder of Christian Science. Noor's father shared his love of music with his children. All the children grew up playing the veena, a stringed instrument from India; the harp; and other instruments.

Noor entered school when she was seven years old. Her family life was so intellectual and serious that she didn't know how to play with other girls. She did make a close friend she would know all her life, but her younger brother, Vilayat, was her best friend, and she was also comfortable being alone.

While on a trip to his homeland of India, Noor's father died unexpectedly, and her mother plunged into a four-year depression. Noor took over managing the household and raising the younger children, a big responsibility for a thirteen-year-old, but she accepted it without question. She continued her schooling, and if she had any free time, she read. Joan of Arc, a national heroine in France who fought and died for her beliefs five hundred years earlier, became her personal heroine.

Noor eventually graduated from the Sorbonne, a famous university in Paris. She was just beginning her career as a children's book author in 1940 when the Germans invaded France. As they marched toward Paris, Noor sat with Vilayat discussing the war. As Sufis, they were taught to accept everyone, even people they disagreed with but, in a flash, both realized they wanted the Nazi atrocities to be stopped. They would do anything to help. They left Paris with thousands of people, and fled to England, since they held British passports, to join the war effort.

Noor studied nursing with the Red Cross, but that didn't feel like enough. She entered the British Women's Auxiliary Air Force and trained to be a wireless radio operator, sending and receiving messages from British bombers on their missions.

Because of her skill with the radio set and her ability to speak French, she came to the notice of officials at Military Intelligence. One day she was summoned to the War Office and asked if she would risk working in Paris for the SOE. The official made it clear that if she were caught by the Gestapo, she could be tortured or even executed.

Noor didn't need to think twice before saying yes.

In training, Noor learned to transmit in code and also to fire a gun, to sneak through the countryside, and to stand up to harsh interrogation. With the cover name Jeanne-Marie Renier to go with her new identity as a nanny, and a code name to use on her transmissions, Madeleine arrived in Paris. Unfortunately, within ten days, many members of her network had been arrested. With lots of the safe houses now compromised, Noor had to find new places to set up her wireless. She contacted French Resistance workers to get information about parachute drops of food and cargo, agents who needed to escape from France, and what the Germans were planning next.

Noor transmitted messages at least four times a day, each time from a different apartment in a different part of Paris. She was always on the run because wireless operators couldn't transmit for more than thirty minutes at a time for fear the Gestapo, driving up and down the streets with detectors, would pinpoint their location. Friends who saw her wondered if she ever had time to eat or sleep. When she did have a chance to sit and talk for a few minutes, she usually dozed off.

In her search for safe houses, Noor even went to Suresnes. She was always in disguise; her hair might be red one day and bleached blond the next. She always wore dark glasses. Still, the people in her old neighborhood recognized her. "Was she afraid?" they asked. She wasn't. She had a calm certainty that those who knew her would never betray her.

Other agents continued to be arrested. One day, her contact Gieules missed a meeting with her. She telephoned him and detected something strange about his voice while he set up another meeting. She spoke to an agent she trusted who went alone and spotted Gieules on a park bench, surrounded by Nazi agents. Noor had narrowly escaped capture.

When one of the apartments Noor used was searched, another agent put her on a train to Normandy, where he found a safe place for Noor to hide. Two days later, he saw her back in Paris. She just would not give up. If anything, she worked harder, moving relentlessly about the city searching for places from which to transmit her messages.

Then it happened. An acquaintance of the landlady at one of Noor's apartments sold information of her whereabouts to the Gestapo. An officer was waiting inside the door one afternoon. He grabbed her. She bit him, fighting desperately. She was tiny, barely over five feet tall, but she put up such a fight that he had retreated and was standing across the room from her, gun drawn, when other officers he'd called to help him arrived.

At Gestapo headquarters she asked to use the bathroom, and the next thing the officials knew, she'd gone out the window and was running across the roof.

Caught again, she was questioned daily, but she wasn't tortured by the Gestapo in Paris. In fact, the officials came to respect her bravery and gentility. They gave her pen and paper, and she spent her time writing and reading. She was able to communicate with other prisoners. During another escape attempt, the air-raid siren went off to announce German bombers were attacking, and the guards saw her and two others on the roof. The official in charge ordered her to sign a statement that she'd never try to escape again. She replied that she'd do anything to escape and go back to spying. This time he sent her to a prison in Germany, where her hands were chained to her feet.

Months passed and on September 12, 1944, Noor and three other women prisoners were taken to the concentration camp at Dachau and executed. Noor was posthumously awarded the George Cross by the British and the Croix de Guerre by the French for her heroic service.

The night Noor died, both her mother and her brother Vilayat had a dream about her. They both described that "Noor appeared to them in uniform, her happy face surrounded by blue light. She told them she was free."[1]

Spy Close-up
Noor's Jataka Tales

Noor Inayat Khan's active imagination helped her in her spy work. As a child, she believed she saw fairies, and she made up stories, songs, and poems about all kinds of things. As she grew up, she got to know a children's illustrator, Baroness van Tuyll, who used the professional name of Harriet Willebeek Le Mair. The baroness asked Noor to work on a book project with her. Noor picked from some of the five hundred legends of Buddha's reincarnations in various animal forms during which he taught lessons of self-sacrifice. Together, the baroness and Noor published *Twenty Jataka Tales* in 1939.

"The Fairy and the Hare" was Noor's favorite story. In it, the hare offers to give himself to a starving old beggar so he could eat. At once, it is revealed that the starving old man is really the fairy Sakka. The fairy tells the hare, "The kindness of your heart, O blessed one, shall be known throughout the world for ages to come."[2]

Like the hare, Noor is known throughout the world for her great kindness and the courage she had in sacrificing herself to spy for freedom.

Create a Cover

When just being herself can give her away, one of the ways a spy can protect herself is to create a new life story. Many of the spies in this book received this training. In her work in France, Noor Inayat Khan, who in real life was a children's author, became Jeanne-Marie Renier, a children's nanny. Her made-up father was Auguste Renier, a professor of philosophy at Princeton who was killed in World War I. Her made-up mother was American-born Ray Baker.

Noor developed family stories about her made-up self. She had lived in France long enough to speak the language without an accent, and she knew her way around. Still, when she first arrived in Paris, one of her team members was horrified to see Noor put milk into her cup, and then add the tea. That was the British way! The French poured the tea first, and then added milk. The enemy would spot that instantly.

What kind of cover story could you make up using some details from your own life and some made-up details taken from things you have read about or experienced? Write your new "biography" using this information:

New Name:_____

New Parents' Names and Occupations: _____

New Siblings: _____

New Birthdate and Place:_____

New Schools: _____

New Hobbies and Talents: _____

New Vacations with Your Family:_____

Now try it out! Give friends your background and have them quiz you about it. See how smooth your answers are. Are there any gaps in your story?

BETTY
PACK

Code Name
Cynthia
1910–1963

B *etty knew that stealing the naval codes would be difficult, but not impossible. She was ready. Shortly after midnight, she and her friend, Charles, walked to the French Vichy Embassy, which was pro-Nazi, and opened the front door with Charles's key. They talked softly in the reception room. When a guard came to investigate, Betty quickly embraced Charles. The guard, seeing what appeared to be two lovers, muttered an apology and left.*

Betty hurried to the door of the naval intelligence office and started to pick open the padlock, just as she had practiced so many times. Her hands shook as she worked the lock. Stay calm, *she reminded herself.* Concentrate. *The lock popped open. Then Betty opened a window to let in an OSS safecracker. In minutes, the safecracker opened the door to the safe and removed the codebooks. He climbed back out the window, down the ladder, and into a waiting car. The car whisked him to a hotel where an OSS team was set up to photograph the codes.*

Betty and Charles anxiously waited for the safecracker to return with the books. The deadline was 4:00 in the morning. By 4:30, no one had appeared. Something had gone wrong.

Betty was born Amy Elizabeth Thorpe in November 1910 in Minneapolis, Minnesota. Her father, George, was an ambitious Marine Corps officer, and her mother, Cora, was a well-educated, worldly person interested in good manners and being active in society. Betty had a younger sister, Jane, and a brother, George.

When Betty's father retired from the military, he took his family on a tour of Europe. Then they settled in Washington, DC, where her father practiced maritime law. They became prominent members of Washington society.

Betty grew up to be a beautiful and slender young woman with reddish-blond hair and green eyes. She attended Wellesley College in Massachusetts, where she studied music. Betty had a mind of her own and, although she was raised to be a debutante, she thought that Washington, DC, society was silly and superficial.

To the surprise of her family, at twenty-one Betty married an older man named Arthur Pack, a diplomat who worked at the British Embassy in Washington, DC. After their marriage, Arthur was transferred to the British Embassy in Chile and then to Spain.

Betty was thrilled to be in Europe with her husband and daughter, but she was often lonely and bored. While they were in Spain, a civil war broke out between the Communists and Nationalists. When the embassy moved from Madrid, Betty and her family moved to Biarritz, just across the French border. One day, Betty met five young revolutionary soldiers. They asked Betty to help them get away from the Communist-held areas before they were caught. Betty didn't hesitate. She loaded them into her car and drove them to France, right through the enemy checkpoints. Because of her diplomatic license plate, she wasn't stopped. This adventure stirred Betty up. She wanted to do more to help the causes she believed in.

The Packs were transferred again, this time to the British Embassy in Warsaw, Poland. War in Europe was about to erupt. Hitler had already

Spy Files

The wristwatch camera dates from 1948. That camera took eight pictures the size of a little fingernail.

conquered Austria and was eyeing Czechoslovakia. Poland was in the middle of it all.

At embassy dinners and receptions, Betty often overheard important information. One evening she heard about Poland's secret plans to deal with Hitler. Betty told everything she had heard to a British official at the embassy. The official revealed that he was part of MI6, Britain's secret intelligence agency abroad, and he asked Betty to get more information for him. A spy was born!

Betty's job was to do lots of entertaining, widen her circle of contacts, and then charm highly placed officials into talking too much. Betty loved the idea of being a spy and helping the Allied cause. The work was challenging, and she was no longer bored. When Arthur was reassigned to Chile, Betty decided not to go. There was little to spy on in Chile, so she returned to the United States alone.

It wasn't long before MI6 contacted Betty again. She was officially recruited into their service under the code name Cynthia, and she was to operate in the Washington, DC, area. On one mission she arranged to meet the naval diplomat of the Italian Embassy. The diplomat fell in love with Betty and, before long, gave her the Italian naval codes. The Allies read the codes, which allowed the British fleet to win a decisive victory over the Italian Navy in 1941 in the Mediterranean.

The British wanted the French Vichy naval codes next. The Allies were planning to invade Vichy territory in North Africa, so the codebooks might prove invaluable. It was Betty's biggest assignment yet. Could she pull it off?

At the French Vichy Embassy in Washington, DC, Betty met Charles Brousse, a French diplomat who worked there. She hoped to convince Charles to help her. Despite working with the Vichy French, Charles detested the Germans and was pro-British. Charles wanted to help Betty, but the codes were in an embassy vault that he did not have access to. They were contained in two dictionary-thick volumes, locked

Spy Files

Boots with rubber soles in the shape of bare feet disguise footprints on beaches and in deserts.

in a safe inside a padlocked room. The embassy was patrolled by an armed watchman and a vicious guard dog. In addition, the Vichy secret police might be watching. But then the American OSS offered to help, and a daring plan was hatched—a plan to steal, photograph, and return the codebooks, all in just a few hours.

Things went as planned until the 4:00 AM deadline was missed. Where was the safecracker with the stolen books?

Finally, at 4:40, he appeared! The team at the hotel had taken longer than expected to photograph the codes. The safecracker climbed back up the ladder, returned the codebooks to the safe, shut everything up again, and disappeared out the window. Betty and Charles calmly left the embassy and walked to the hotel.

Several months later, the Allies launched Operation Torch, the invasion of French North Africa. The Nazis were taken completely by surprise. Six months later, all of North Africa was in Allied control, thanks in part to the courage and daring of Cynthia.

After her success at the French Vichy Embassy, Betty retired from spying. She and Charles had fallen deeply in love. Betty divorced Arthur and married Charles, and they moved to an old French chateau in the Pyrenees Mountains.

Years later, Betty grew seriously ill with cancer. Before she died, she wrote her autobiography and many articles about her life as a spy.

Spy Files

When spies break into a building to plant a bug, they sometimes take their own dust along to replace the dust they may disturb on a table, desk, or windowsill.

The Chinese Revolution

(1949)

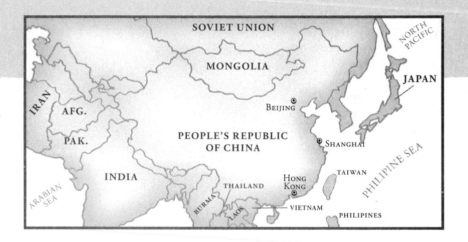

During World War II, the Nationalists and Communists in China joined together to fight against fascist forces, chiefly the Japanese. But afterward, they continued their long-lasting internal war for control of China.

The Nationalists were at this time the governing party. While they held a much larger territory and enjoyed more support from other countries, mainly the United States, they suffered from corruption and a lack of troop morale. They were no match for the disciplined and well-formed communist Peoples Liberation Army. The Nationalist party, led by Chiang Kai-shek, was driven out of mainland China to Taiwan by the Communists, who were backed by the Soviet Union.

In 1949, China became the People's Republic of China. Pockets of resistance remained. The Nationalists tried to rid their country of Communists, and secret agents were needed. Women played a role. They had taken on the cover of stage performers many times before. It would work again.

EVA WU

Daring Dancer

CIRCA 1934-?

*E*va *turned toward her audience to begin dancing. Her heart started to pound. The policemen who had questioned her earlier that afternoon entered the room. There too, on the other side of the room, was her contact, a Nationalist secret agent. Wound in Eva's hair was a white chrysanthemum, a signal to the agent that her latest mission had gone well.*

With the Communist police at her show, she should have been wearing a red flower to warn the agent that danger was nearby. How could she change the white flower to red?

Eva Wu was born in China around 1934. Not much is known about her childhood, except that she was one of fifteen children. Her father was a wealthy doctor in Canton.

In 1949 the Communist party came into power. Eva's father feared that the Communists would take all of his money, so he dispersed his family, giving each member a small amount of gold—enough to get settled somewhere away from Canton.

Eva made her way to Hong Kong, which was at that time a British colony. She became a dancer at a cosmopolitan nightclub. People from all over the world came to see her dance. One of her most famous performances was a temple dance to keep away evil spirits. In one hand, Eva carried a jade-handled dagger and in the other, a bowl of water. With graceful gestures, Eva gave the impression that she was purifying herself, the audience, and all of the land around them. At the end of the dance, the audience often sat silently entranced, so enchanting was Eva's beauty and the movements of her dance.

Spy Files

A microdot is a photo negative the size of the period at the end of this sentence. With the help of a microscope, an agent can read every word on the microdot.

While Eva enjoyed dancing, she wondered how she could help rid her country of the Communists. Her answer came one night in the form of a stranger who met with her after the show. He asked if she would like to serve her country.

Eva agreed to help the stranger, who was really a secret agent for the Nationalist Party. He explained to Eva that her missions would be simple: She would serve as a courier, smuggling messages out of Hong Kong into nearby Kowloon, a Communist-held city. She already had the perfect disguise—a dancer browsing the shops in Kowloon for silks, brocades, and perfumes. To find out how her mission went, the intelligence officer would attend her shows. If all had gone well, Eva would wear a white chrysanthemum in her hair. If she needed to warn him, the flower would be red.

On Eva's first mission, she hid a written message in her mass of shiny black hair, which she arranged in loops. During an "innocent" shopping expedition in Kowloon, Eva easily passed the letter to a shopkeeper, another Nationalist agent.

On later missions, Eva's reports were hidden on microfilm. Anyone watching this delicate-looking dancer finger a swatch of silk or buy a new costume would never have suspected her of transferring spy documents. Yet Eva became an important undercover courier in that area for Chiang Kai-shek's espionage system.

For months, everything went smoothly. Eva felt proud that she was helping in this small way. As an added bonus, the intelligence officer gave her information on the whereabouts of some of her family members who were still in Communist China.

One day while shopping, she was stopped by the Communist police. They had suspected Eva for some time and insisted on searching her. They took her to a police station where a woman searched her and all of her belongings. She found nothing and let Eva go. But Eva was carrying a message. It was hidden in a microdot as small as a pinpoint, placed on the inside of one of her hairpins. Once out of sight of the police, Eva delivered the microscopic message.

That evening when Eva stepped onto the stage, she hadn't expected to see the policemen. She realized that the Communists must still suspect her. Did they know her contact was at the show? If seen together, she and the other agent would be arrested. As the music to the purification dance began, it came to her. She knew how to warn her contact right under the noses of the Communist officers. She would simply add a new ending to the dance.

As the dance ended, Eva slowly kneeled and placed the brass bowl on the floor before her. She took the dagger from her sash and cut a long gash down the length of her arm. With a dramatic gesture, she ran the white chrysanthemum along the dripping wound, and then held the blood-red flower above her head. She smiled. The audience was spellbound by the new ending.

Eva's contact was not. He knew there was trouble. After the performance, he met her at a side door, and they slipped into the night. Eva never danced at the nightclub again.

No one is sure where Eva and her contact went. Some say she traveled to Taiwan, where she joined some of her brothers. She may, or may not, be alive today. But whatever happened to Eva Wu, no one will ever forget the courage of this daring dancer.

How Observant Are You?

S pies need to be observant. They need to know if they're being followed. They might have to recount details of a particular place. Spies need to be able to sense which people they can trust.

How observant are you? Play this game with a friend and find out. One of you will guess what the other has changed about her appearance. All you need is a watch or clock with a second hand and concentration.

1. Sit opposite your friend and for 10 seconds look at her closely.
2. Now close your eyes for 20 seconds.
3. While your eyes are closed, your friend should change one thing about her appearance.
4. She will alert you to open your eyes once the 20 seconds are complete. You should then study your friend to determine what has changed in her appearance. Did she take an earring off? Add a bracelet? Untuck part of her blouse?
5. Switch, and now it's her turn to guess while you make the changes.

You can make the game more challenging by increasing the number of changes with each turn. Or focus on subtle changes, such as turning around a ring or placing a hand in a new position. Even add changes that indicate behavior, such as looking sad or squinting.

If more than two people play, some can make one or more changes, while the others figure them out, either separately or as a team. If the observers leave the room, furniture and fixtures can be moved too. The possibilities are endless. And you'll hone your observations skills. You never know when you're going to need them . . .

The Cold War
(CIRCA 1945–1991)

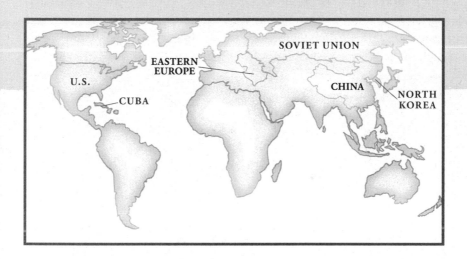

The Cold War started between the Soviet Union and the United States when the Soviet Union set up Communist governments in the Eastern European countries they liberated during World War II (East Germany, Poland, Hungary, Bulgaria, Czechoslovakia, Romania, Albania, and Yugoslavia). Neither side physically fought each other, but they took opposite sides as other countries fought within their borders and between each other. The United States was concerned with the spread of Communism. Both sides were concerned with the spread of nuclear weapons.

Spying focused on acquiring knowledge of what the other side was doing and planning. Agents turned into double agents or even triple agents! No one could be trusted. Secret codes, miniature cameras, dead drops, obscure drugs, and spy dust were all part of an array of Cold War spycraft.

Communist spy networks were directed against many Western countries. The United States responded by creating the Central Intelligence Agency (CIA), the National Security Agency (NSA), and the Defense Intelligence Agency (DIA). Knowing what the other side was thinking could often help head off a "hot war," a fight with weapons.

In this era of mistrust, women found many opportunities to spy. Computers and satellites provided exciting new ways to collect intelligence. Some women worked as technicians and analysts in these new technology-driven intelligence-gathering operations. Some rose to the highest ranks in management. Others developed sources of information or operated in elaborately staged espionage missions where masters of disguise were vital to their success.

JONNA
HIESTAND
MENDEZ

Disguise Master

1945–

*Jonna worked her magic. The slight, clean-shaven man with the
birthmark on his face was gone. In his place stood an older, gray-
haired, mustached fellow with glasses and a smooth complexion. But
would the clever disguise be good enough to steal KAPELLE?*

Jonna Hiestand was born in 1945 in Campbellsville, Kentucky, and
grew up in Kansas. Both of her parents worked for Boeing Aircraft, her
father as a mechanic and her mother in the computer sector. Jonna was
one of four daughters.

As a girl, Jonna was quiet but independent. She liked school and
especially enjoyed studying languages and foreign cultures. Being shy
didn't stop her from getting into mischief—like pouring liquid soap
into the town fountain. Jonna got a taste of travel early on when her
family piled into the car for cross-country trips to visit relatives.

Jonna also liked art, particularly painting and photography. She later
explained, "Throughout my career, these interests seemed to guide me.
I became a professional photographer, instructing foreign agents around

the world. When I went into the field of disguise, it was my knowledge of art, colors, mediums, and composition that gave my work an original dimension. A good eye is important in the disguise field."[1]

In 1966, while living in Europe, Jonna met a young group of professionals who turned out to be CIA officers. Jonna found her new friends intriguing and applied to the agency. At first she worked for the CIA overseas as a secretary. She then continued in Washington, DC, rising up through the ranks to become a technical operations officer and, finally, the CIA's chief of disguise.

The CIA sent Jonna on assignments overseas in 1987. Her area of operation covered territory from Pakistan to Burma, and from Sri Lanka to the Himalayas. Jonna was part of a unit that could do just about anything. Need to break into an office? Steal a codebook? Photograph a document? No problem. What Jonna and her team could accomplish wasn't far off from the capers in a James Bond movie.

For Operation KAPELLE, a plan to steal a top-secret Soviet communications device, the team would be working within a local population, and the members needed to blend in perfectly. This would demand Jonna's best disguise work.

Jonna and the team leader, Cooper, drove to a hotel in the center of town where they rented a room with a view of their target: the Soviet compound. The room would serve as their observation post. One of Jonna's first jobs was to take photographs of the compound.

From Cooper, she learned that this Soviet compound was short staffed. Many people were on vacation, so the security wouldn't be tight. She also learned that the KAPELLE device was inside an especially secure room called the Sanctum.

The Sanctum was built like a bank vault with thick walls and a huge metal door. No key could open this door. It was locked with dead bolts and combination locks. Inside the Sanctum, the team would find the KAPELLE bolted to the floor. Taking the KAPELLE would be a "smoking bolt operation" (CIA slang for describing the swiftness of a snatch, as in "There was nothing left but the smoking bolts on the floor").[2]

A local CIA agent, code name TUGBOAT, was to help them get into the building, but he needed a disguise—one that would give him a new look, yet allow him to blend in on the street. TUGBOAT had already taken big risks working on other jobs for the CIA. People knew him in town. He'd need to be unrecognizable to help with the KAPELLE job. When they met, Jonna was distressed to see a large birthmark running down the right side of his face. How could she cover that up?

Jonna needed a lot of disguise materials to begin transforming TUGBOAT. She got cosmetics from case officers' wives—foundation, powder, eyeliner, eyebrow pencil, anything. She also asked the staff to pool their disguise kits, which were issued to each case officer before he or she left for an overseas assignment.

The next day Jonna met TUGBOAT in a safe house. She picked through the pile of cosmetics heaped on the dining room table—even a can of Dr. Scholl's foot powder might prove useful. She lined up applicators, towels, a brush, a comb, and a mirror. Then she sat TUGBOAT down in a chair and got to work.

One hour later, Jonna was done. Another intelligence officer who knew TUGBOAT hardly recognized him. TUGBOAT was ready.

In his new disguise, TUGBOAT approached the guard at the Soviet compound, showed him a fake police ID card (another one of Jonna's tricks), and explained that he was conducting a routine check of all the locks on the buildings. The guard hesitated, but opened the gate when TUGBOAT handed him a roll of money.

Once inside, TUGBOAT made careful measurements of the locks on the outer doors. He took them back to the snatch team, which cut a key to fit each lock.

The team was just about ready to move. Jonna checked everyone's disguises and insisted that they practice their new identities, walking and driving around town until they felt comfortable in their covers.

Spy Files

Spy satellites orbiting Earth 250 miles away can make out objects as small as a grapefruit.

On the night of the operation, the whole Soviet staff was away at a hunting camp. It was cool and the humidity had lessened—good for keeping the disguises intact. Jonna's team traveled to the compound and stopped at the gate. The guard believed the disguised TUGBOAT was bringing in a team of security experts to do a surprise inspection of the compound. TUGBOAT gave the guard another roll of money, and the guard opened the gate and left. The van backed up to the central building and the snatch began.

The mission went like clockwork. The snatch team got through the outer doors with the new keys. The specially locked door inside gave the spies no problems, either. The entry team had a special device, PLASMA, that fired a tiny explosive through the door and severed the lock mechanism, allowing the door to be opened immediately. The team removed KAPELLE from the Soviet stronghold, slipped it into the van, and drove it out of the country—all in less than twenty-four hours. Everyone's cover remained intact, thanks to Jonna's skill.

Jonna continued to work overseas on other assignments, developing her disguise magic. In one of her last operations, she teamed up with Tony Mendez, a previous chief of disguise for the CIA, to head a group of officers in a risky and complicated plan to help a Russian source escape Moscow. Later, Jonna and Tony married.

Now they are both retired from the CIA and live in Maryland. Jonna, a professional photographer and author, is on the board of directors for the International Spy Museum in Washington, DC. She has lectured with her husband at the Joint Military Intelligence College, World Affairs Councils, and colleges and universities.

Of her career, Jonna says:

Young teens in today's somewhat overwhelming society might find it interesting to realize that one person can still make a difference in the world. A lot of my work gave me a steady sense of satisfaction that I think few jobs can provide. Some lives were protected, some threats overcome, and the United States benefited. I left the work feeling that it had been worthwhile. I made a contribution when it counted. What more can we hope for? I am so proud to have been part of the history of the Cold War and the years immediately after.[3]

STELLA RIMINGTON'S PERSISTENCE

Dame Stella Rimington began her Security Service (MI5) career in 1967 in India. She traveled there as the wife of a diplomat and started working as an assistant to one of the United Kingdom's First Secretaries of the High Commission. When she returned to London, she continued working for MI5 full-time. Dame Stella soon realized that it was her dream career, but she knew it would be an uphill battle. She would have to fight the perception that women were not suited for certain roles, such as meeting intelligence sources in the field. Dame Stella persisted, even when she became a single parent.

She worked her way up through the ranks and in December 1991, following a trip to Moscow to reestablish relations with the KGB after the Cold War ended, she was named the director-general. She was MI5's first female head. Dame Stella oversaw counterterrorism, counterespionage, and countersubversion. She strove for a policy of greater openness, believing that the public should know more about MI5 and the extent of its responsibilities. She was the first leader whose name was made public during her term.

Since her retirement in 1996, Dame Stella has conducted research at various archives throughout the UK, archive preservation being the focus of her first job when she graduated from the University of Liverpool. She's turned her research and inside information about the workings of spy operations into a series of thriller novels featuring the fictional MI5 officer Liz Carlyle.

A Changing World
(1992–TODAY)

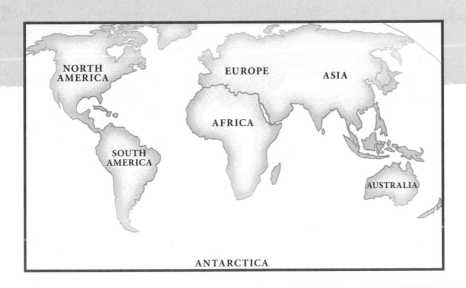

NORTH AMERICA

EUROPE

ASIA

AFRICA

SOUTH AMERICA

AUSTRALIA

ANTARCTICA

Though tensions often ran high during the Cold War, the superpowers of the United States and the Soviet Union, along with their allies, achieved an overall balance. By the late 1980s, agreements to curb the nuclear arms race were signed. Then reforms in the Soviet Union led to demands by other Communist countries for free elections. Communism collapsed in Eastern Europe, and the Berlin Wall was taken down. By 1991, the Cold War was over.

But with the end of the Cold War, new world contours emerged and with them, new levels of uncertainty and conflict. Countries are increasingly tied together economically, yet many developing countries are unstable because of high levels of poverty and low levels of education. New democratic governments have taken the place of dictatorships around the world, but many are fraught with ethnic, cultural, and religious tension. Countries can't necessarily count on longtime allies.

Spy services in countries throughout the world must be focused everywhere, though the United States has specific challenges following the 9/11 attacks. The spread of nuclear weapons is again a world concern. And economic spying is rampant.

Spies continue to play an important role in shaping the world. Both human and electronic intelligence—including computers, satellites, and drones—assist governments in creating appropriate diplomatic and military strategy. Women continue to be there, working in high-level positions within the military and intelligence agencies, both at home and as operatives abroad, to stand up for the cause of freedom.

Spotlight:
VALERIE PLAME WILSON, BETRAYED

S pies need to operate in secret. Their work can be dangerous to themselves and to others. So what are the consequences when a spy's identity is revealed?

This happened to Valerie Plame Wilson, a CIA officer who worked in the CIA's Counterproliferation Division in the early 2000s. While assigned to the division, she tracked the growth of nuclear programs in various parts of the world. She traveled under nonofficial cover (NOC), which means she didn't work as a diplomat or in another government job. Instead, she worked in businesses without government ties. Being an NOC carries extra danger. If NOCs are caught spying, they don't have immunity.

Overseas, Valerie worked in several NOC jobs, including as an energy analyst. She met with workers in the nuclear industry, cultivated sources, and managed the work of other spies.

In 2003, a *Washington Post* column identified her as a CIA operative. Her cover blown, Valerie left the CIA. However, consequences reached beyond ending her career. The US government's ability to track nuclear weapons was damaged. Leaking her name exposed the identity of a CIA front company, also an NOC, and to what extent the people working there were endangered isn't known.

In an interview on NBC's *TODAY* in 2007, Valerie said, "I do know that the network of assets I worked with is jeopardized. That's why what happened was a real crime of violence against our national security."[1]

Valerie now lives in Santa Fe, New Mexico, where she works at an independent scientific think tank.

Orienteering

Can you follow directions to a place you've never been before? During their training, CIA officers do land navigation exercises to help prepare them to track someone or something or to escape through unfamiliar territory. Lindsay Moran found this to be one of the most challenging parts of her training.

Want to practice this skill? Try the sport of orienteering. If you are a Girl Scout, you can earn the Finding Your Way badge. You'll follow trails, read maps, and head out for your destination. And you'll get more involved with the world around you: hilly or flat, muddy or dry, full of wildlife or so quiet, you can hear a branch break.

Meanwhile, you might want to try a Treasure or Scavenger Hunt in your neighborhood!

1. Figure out your course.
2. Hide clues at spots along the way. (An example of a written clue: *Now go to the third tree from the front fence in Ms. Fletcher's backyard and look up high.*)
3. Have each clue lead to the next clue.
4. Play in teams or as individuals.
5. Make the treasure into a picnic or treat for all.

If you know how to use a compass, another idea for your treasure hunt is to use compass coordinates instead of providing written clues for your friends to find the next spot. (An example of a compass coordinate clue: 49° N, 122°W, look up high.)

Just be sure to ask "Ms. Fletcher" first!

LINDSAY
MORAN

On Her Own
1969—

Certain no one was spying on her, Lindsay bicycled up a winding mountain road to the signal site at the top. She needed to let her agent know she wanted to meet him the next morning to see if he knew the National Liberation Army's next target.

Just before her final steep ascent, three camouflaged, armed figures strode brashly down the middle of the road. The short one had a Macedonian flag patch on his jacket, but Lindsay couldn't be sure they weren't rebels disguised in their victims' clothing. Would they let her pass unchallenged? Focusing straight ahead, she pedaled onward, feeling their eyes on her back and hearing derisive laughter.

She made it to the top, marked the concrete water well with a charcoal slash, and hoped her agent was still unafraid to venture to the site.

Rounding a turn on her descent, she saw the same short soldier dive into brush at the side of the road. She jammed on her brakes, but how could she outrace them pedaling back uphill? Willing her voice to be calm, she called out, "Excuse me!"

In response, she heard the click of a trigger being cocked.[1]

Lindsay Moran felt she'd spent her childhood training to be a spy. She grew up thinking her father's top-secret projects at his job in Washington, DC, and her grandfather's jobs all over the world meant they were spies (though she later learned this was a mistaken assumption). She poured over *Harriet the Spy* books, sent coded messages by flashlight to her friend in a nearby house, and arranged her clothing in special ways so she could tell if someone had searched her suitcase when traveling with her father.

As she got older, she read James Bond novels and CIA memoirs. Though her father told her the CIA would never take her because she'd experimented with drugs during her college years at Harvard, she sent a résumé the day after her college graduation. It wasn't till five years later, after attending graduate school in New York, teaching English in Bulgaria, and teaching writing at a community college in San Francisco, that Lindsay decided to actually apply. Her family and her boyfriend had the same concerns: her lifestyle was too liberal; she wouldn't be happy in a male-dominated organization; she'd withdraw from them because of the need to be secretive.

After multiple interviews and a polygraph test, she was accepted. At the same time, she received a Fulbright scholarship to return to Bulgaria. It would give her one last year of freedom and help deepen her knowledge of the language and culture in that Eastern European country, and the CIA agreed to defer her admission.

One of the hardest exercises Lindsay went through once she began her official training at The Farm, the CIA's field academy outside Williamsburg, Virginia, was the land navigation exercise. After a few hours of classroom instruction, the class members were given a compass and two light sticks. In the middle of the night, they were transported into nearby woods with the goal of finding their way to their own set of compass coordinates, each a separate spot about a mile away.

The undergrowth was so dense, the night so dark. Any crackle of leaves filled Lindsay's mind with images of snakes about to coil around her leg or cougars ready to spring. After what seemed to be hours, she was sure she couldn't go another step. Then she pictured the teasing she'd receive from classmates if she had to be rescued, and she pushed on. What pride she felt knowing she was actually one of the first to find her checkpoint. Even more important: She'd overcome near-paralyzing fear.

Her year of training included tackling obstacle courses, parachuting, practicing evasive driving, crashing through barriers, and experiencing pepper spray firsthand. She learned traditional spy techniques, too, like using a dead drop or a signal site, coding messages, and avoiding surveillance.

Early in Lindsay's training, she worked as a reports officer. Her job was to remove from documents anything that might reveal the identity of an agent. Agents are local recruits who help with missions and provide invaluable information about their city or country. Lindsay's reports came from case officers working in and around Skopje, the capital of the Republic of Macedonia, which became independent when Yugoslavia was divided up after the Cold War ended. Perhaps because of that job, and because of her experiences in the neighboring country of Bulgaria, Lindsay was sent to Skopje as a case officer.

She began to develop several contacts of her own, but she never felt completely sure what kind of intelligence she was getting. Her boss would meet periodically with his case officers, and check in with her individually, but she was basically on her own.

She could never relax. Was she being followed? Was her apartment bugged? Her phone tapped? She began to be suspicious of everyone. And she was lonely. She had friends, Emily and Emma, Americans who were living in Bulgaria, and she'd drive there occasionally to be with them. But she could never really tell them what she was doing, never ask for advice, never tell heartwarming or funny workplace stories.

Other former Yugoslav republics had experienced bloody civil wars and ethnic cleansing, and Albanian forces in the National Liberation Army (NLA) began to act up against the predominantly Slav population. Over a period of months, villages were shelled, landmines exploded, firefights erupted in the hills. When a Macedonian police station was bombed, killing several more people, Lindsay's boss wanted her to meet with her most promising Albanian agent to see what inside information he might have. She headed up the mountain to mark their signal site. On her way back home, she was ambushed by armed soldiers, and she wasn't sure whose side they were on.

She shouted, "Excuse me," followed by a Macedonian insult, the kind men used to tease each other. For long seconds nothing happened.

Then the three soldiers realized she must be on their side. They filed out of the bushes, and she discovered they really were Macedonian. She chatted long enough to learn one of the men wanted to go to America. She'd found someone else she might trade with: a visa for information. She soon recruited him.

Though hostilities between the NLA and the Macedonian government were eventually resolved, a new worry came from the Lions, a rogue Macedonian police force filled with criminals. It turned out that Lindsay's new recruit, Tony, had an important contact in the Lions and she began meeting with him.

In the middle of this activity, on the other side of the ocean from Lindsay, a terrorist group staged attacks on the World Trade Center towers in New York City. Americans were in shock.

Lindsay was haunted by the thought that the organization she worked for had not been able to get information to prevent that from happening. She continued her work in Skopje but grew frustrated when things seemed to move so slowly, and she opposed the war in Iraq.

She officially resigned from the CIA in 2003, and several months later married James Kegley, a man she'd met during the break between her training and her deployment to Skopje. They now have young children, and Lindsay writes articles and gives talks on a variety of subjects, including her CIA service.

While Lindsay concluded that being a spy was not something she could continue, she says, "I believe the CIA has one of the most important missions in our government. The Agency will always require bright and motivated young people to pursue and fulfill that mission. Simply put, every country needs a spy service, and ours should be the best."[2]

Spy Files

In the early 1970s, solar energy powered a bug hidden in a tree stump near Moscow. The "green" bug intercepted signals from a nearby Soviet air base, and then beamed them to a satellite, which then sent them to a site in the United States. Solar power meant no batteries were needed to keep the bug going.

Get Ready for Your Spy Career!

T hinking about becoming a spy? You'll need a résumé
that will impress seasoned CIA officers. Here's a list of
skills, knowledge, and attitudes you might start checking off
now. Actually, this list will prepare you for lots of careers.

____ Be adventurous.

____ Stay fit.

____ Learn at least one foreign language.

____ Take an overseas semester or a year abroad.

____ Experience other cultures through people, movies,
books, and travel.

____ Read the news of world events.

____ Get to know your computer, inside and out.

____ Develop social media and other networking skills,
and know what to keep private.

____ Know a little chemistry.

____ Camp out, read maps, follow trails.

____ Try acting.

____ Practice different disguises and try changing your
everyday look.

____ Study our Constitution.

____ Stay within the law.

____ Stand up for yourself.

____ Think about what you believe in and what you would
fight for.

____ Set your sights high.

____ Add some goals of your own!

Afterword

Television shows, movies, and books often portray spying as a glamorous profession. You might dream of this life of adventure! Think twice. Along with the thrills, there's real danger. As you've seen, spies can be caught, imprisoned, and even executed.

Being a secret agent isn't for everyone, but standing up for what you believe is something you can do. We hope the stories in this book will inspire you to be daring and brave and find courage when you need it. One person can make a difference!

Spy Files

The International Spy Museum in Washington, DC, is the only public museum in the United States dedicated solely to espionage. Visit it in Washington, DC, or online at www.spymuseum.org.

Notes

THE AMERICAN REVOLUTION

Lydia Darragh: The Fighting Quaker and Quakers Fight for Freedom (c. 1728–1789)

1. There are differing accounts of Lydia's story: She goes straight home, she goes on to the tavern to make doubly sure the message gets through, or the officer takes her to a nearby farmhouse where she spends the night, possibly sending the lady of the house on to the tavern with the message. Colonel Elias Boudinot, who met with spies at the tavern, wrote in his journal that an old and nondescript woman gave him a message that day, hidden in a needle book. Historians aren't sure which is the most accurate, but all agree that Lydia did overhear the warning and deliver the message.

2. Elizabeth D. Leonard, *All the Daring of the Soldier: Women of the Civil War Armies* (New York: W. W. Norton & Co., 1999), 25.

3. Jean Kinney Williams, *The Quakers* (Danbury, CT: Franklin Watts, 1998).

4. Kate Clifford Larson, *Bound for the Promised Land: Harriet Tubman, Portrait of an American Hero* (New York: Ballantine Books, 2004), 109.

Anna Smith Strong: The Spy in Petticoats (1740–1812)

1. Alexander Rose, *Washington's Spies: The Story of America's First Spy Ring* (New York: Random House, Bantam Books, 2006), 251–59.

Emily Geiger: Caught! (c. 1762–1790)

1. Frank O. Clark, PhD, published a collection of traditional stories and affidavits given by descendants of Emily Geiger in *Emily Geiger, A Set of Source Documents*, online at http://sciway3.net/clark/revolutionarywar/geigeroutline .html. While he cautions that none are valid as original documents, the fact that so many stories have been passed down in the family is a strong indication that Emily Geiger did exist and did perform her service. Both the Geiger family and the Threewits family include her in their genealogy. Their records indicate that Emily Geiger married John Threewits on October 18, 1789, but she died shortly thereafter in childbirth. The child died as well, so Emily had no direct descendants.

Laodicea Langston: Daring Dicey (1766–1837)
1. *The Greenville (SC) Mountaineer*, June 10, 1837, as quoted in EZ Langston, "Laodicea Langston: 'Daring Dicey,'" http://www.ezlangston.com/dicey.html.

Patience Wright: Artist and Spy (1725–1786)
1. George Washington, letter to Mrs. Wright in England, January 30, 1785, as quoted in C. H. Hart, *The Connoisseur*, vol. 19, Sept.–Dec. 1907: 22.

THE WARS OF INDEPENDENCE IN SPANISH AMERICA

Josefa Ortiz de Dominguez: La Heroina (1768–1829)
1. Josefa Ortiz, as quoted in Jerome R. Adams, *Notable Latin American Women: Twenty-nine Leaders, Rebels, Poets, Battlers and Spies, 1500–1900* (Jefferson, NC: McFarland & Co., 1995), 88.

Leona Vicario: Madre de la Patria (1789–1842)
1. Jerome R. Adams, *Notable Latin American Women: Twenty-nine Leaders, Rebels, Poets, Battlers and Spies, 1500–1900* (Jefferson, NC: McFarland & Co., 1995), 118.

Policarpa Salavarrieta: La Pola (1795–1817)
1. There is no birth certificate for Policarpa, but she is called Apolonia in her father's will, and she used the name Gregoria Apolinaria on a forged passport. Perhaps she first used Policarpa when military forces began searching for her. A source list of public records and other documents can be found in "Policarpa Salavarrieta," *Wikipedia, the Free Encyclopedia*. Last modified December 8, 2011. http://en.wikipedia.org/wiki/Policarpa_Salavarrieta.

2. Policarpa Salavarrieta, as quoted in James D. Henderson and Linda Roddy Henderson, *Ten Notable Women of Latin America* (Chicago: Nelson-Hall, Inc., 1978), 119.

THE CIVIL WAR

Harriet Tubman: Without Equal (1822–1913)
1. Two recent biographies of Harriet Tubman have uncovered new public and private records, from interviews with Harriet's relatives, to genealogy websites, to interpretations of traditional stories and legends about Harriet's life and deeds: Kate Clifford Larson, *Bound for the Promised Land: Harriet Tubman, Portrait of an American Hero* (New York: Ballantine Books, 2004) and Jean M. Humez, *Harriet Tubman: The Life and the Life Stories* (Madison: The University of Wisconsin Press, 2003).

2. Harriet Tubman, as quoted in M. W. Taylor, *Harriet Tubman: Antislavery Activist* (Philadelphia: Chelsea House Publishers, 1991), 37.

3. William Still, as quoted in Nancy A. Davidson, "Harriet Tubman, 'Moses,'" in *Notable Black American Women*, ed. Jessie Carney Smith (Detroit: Gale Research, 1992), 1153.

Elizabeth Van Lew: Crazy Bet (1818–1900)

1. William Gilmore Beymer, *On Hazardous Service: Scouts and Spies of the North and South* (New York: Harper & Brothers Publishers, 1912), 78–79.

2. Ibid., 99.

Mary Bowser: From Slave to Spy (c. 1839–?)

1. Elizabeth R. Varon, *Southern Lady, Yankee Spy: The True Story of Elizabeth Van Lew, A Union Agent in the Heart of the Confederacy* (New York: Oxford University Press, Inc., 2003), Chapters 1 and 7 and notes. Varon has done extensive research, piecing together prior conjectures regarding Mary Elizabeth Bowser with information about Mary Jane Rix/Richards, alias Mary Jones. Varon has searched US Federal Census records, baptism (1846) and marriage (1861) records from Richmond, newspaper articles from the period, and personal recollections of Thomas McNiven, another spy in Van Lew's network. Varon has taken a new look at a 1910 interview of Elizabeth Van Lew's niece Annie Randolph (Van Lew) Hall, an interview of Mary J. R. Richards in 1867, and Mary J. R. Richard's personal papers. Varon concludes that while there is no definitive evidence that Mary Elizabeth Bowser and Mary Jane Richards are one and the same, the documents that exist strongly suggest it. Because it is under the name Mary Elizabeth Bowser that the Mary of the various papers is honored in the US Army Military Intelligence Corps Hall of Fame, this is the name used for her in this story.

2. Mary Boykin Chesnut, as quoted in Katherine M. Jones, *Ladies of Richmond, Confederate Capital* (Indianapolis: The Bobbs-Merrill Company, Inc., 1962), p. 195. Jones found the quote in Isabella D. Martin and Myrta Lockett Avary, eds., *A Diary of Dixie* (New York: D. Appleton and Company, 1905).

3. MI Corps Hall of Fame. "Ms. Mary E. Bowser." *Military Intelligence Professional Bulletin*, July–September 1995.

Belle Boyd: La Belle Rebelle (1844–1900)

1. Belle Boyd, *Belle Boyd in Camp and Prison, Written by Herself*, ed. Curtis C. Davis, (New York: Thomas Yoseleff, 1968), 167.

Pauline Cushman: Her Best Role (1833–1893)

1. As quoted by F. L. Sarmiento, *Life of Pauline Cushman* (Philadelphia: John E. Potter & Co., 1865), 62–67.

2. William J. Christen, *Pauline Cushman: Spy of the Cumberland* (Roseville, MN: Edinborough Press, 2006). Christen has done extensive research in census, marriage, birth, and death records; an unpublished scrapbook kept by Pauline; and contemporary newspaper articles in the various cities where Pauline is purported to have lived. He concludes that F. L. Sarmiento, whose book came out when Pauline was performing her Spy of the Cumberland act with P. T.

Barnum, embellished many of the stories in his biography regarding Pauline's childhood, her acting career, and her service. That Pauline served as a spy and scout during the war is confirmed by both books.

WORLD WAR II

Virginia Hall: Wanted! The Limping Lady (1906–1982)

1. Pierre Fayol, as quoted in Elizabeth P. McIntosh, *Sisterhood of Spies* (New York: Dell Publishing, 1998), p. 335. McIntosh found the quote in Pierre Fayol, *Le Chambon-sur-Lignon sous l'occupation, 1940–1944* (Paris: Edition L'Hartmattan, 1990).

2. Ibid.

3. V. Hall, as quoted in Gerald K. Haines, "Virginia Hall Goillot, Career Intelligence Officer," *Prologue Quarterly of the National Archives* 26 no. 4 (Winter 1991): 249–60, http://www.cia.gov/ciakids/history.

Gertrude S. Legendre: Making Her Mark (1902–2000)

1. Gertrude S. Legendre, *The Time of My Life* (Charleston, SC: Wyrick and Company, 1987), 173.

2. Ibid.

Maria Gulovich: Shadow Warrior (1921–2009)

1. OSS personnel files held in the National Archives (NARA RG 226 Entry 108B84F691 Box 84 Folder 691), as quoted by Elizabeth P. McIntosh, *Sisterhood of Spies* (New York: Dell Publishing, 1998), 198.

Josephine Baker: Forever Grateful (1906–1975)

1. Josephine Baker, as quoted in Ean Wood, *The Josephine Baker Story* (London: Sanctuary Publishing Ltd, 2000), 222.

2. Ibid., 214.

3. Ibid., 301.

Noor Inayat Khan: Light of Womanhood (1914–1944) and Noor's Jataka Tales

1. Shrabani Basu, *Spy Princess: The Life of Noor Inayat Khan* (Stroud, UK: Sutton Publishing Limited, 2006), xxii. In her research, Basu had access to SOE personnel files newly released in 2003. This and other facts updated in Noor's story are drawn from Basu's book.

2. Noor Inayat Khan, *Twenty Jataka Tales* (Rochester, VT: Inner Traditions International, 1975), 51.

THE COLD WAR
Jonna Hiestand Mendez: Disguise Master (1945–)

1. Jonna Mendez, email to Elizabeth G. Macalaster, February 11, 2003.

2. Antonio and Jonna Mendez, with Bruce Henderson, *Spy Dust: Two Masters of Disguise Reveal the Tools and Operations that Helped Win the Cold War* (New York: Atria Books, 2002), 63.

3. Jonna Mendez, email to Elizabeth G. Macalaster, February 11, 2003.

A CHANGING WORLD
Valerie Plame Wilson, Betrayed

1. Valerie Plame interviewed by Mike Celizic, "Spy outed in newspaper: 'It was political payback'", NBC's *Today*, October 22, 2007. http://today.msnbc .msn.com/id/21417310/ns/today-today_people/t/spy-outed-newspaper-.

Lindsay Moran: On Her Own (1969–)

1. Lindsay Moran, *Blowing My Cover* (New York: Berkley Books, 2005), 235–38.

2. Lindsay Moran, email to Pamela D. Greenwood, December 30, 2011.

Bibliography

BAKER, JOSEPHINE AND JOSEPHINE'S RAINBOW TRIBE *World War II*

Atwood, Kathryn J. *Women Heroes of World War II: 26 Stories of Espionage, Sabotage, Resistance, and Rescue*. Chicago: Chicago Review Press, 2011.

Baker, Josephine, and Jo Bouillon. *Josephine*. Translated by Mariana Fitzpatrick. New York: Paragon House Publishers, 1988.

Papich, Stephen. *Remembering Josephine*. Indianapolis: Bobbs-Merrill, 1976.

Wood, Ean. *The Josephine Baker Story*. London: Sanctuary Publishing Ltd., 2000.

BEHN, APHRA *The Anglo-Dutch Wars*

Blashfield, Evangeline W. *Portraits and Backgrounds*. New York: Charles Scribner's Sons, 1917.

Goreau, Angeline. *Reconstructing Aphra: A Social Biography of Aphra Behn*. Oxford, UK: Oxford University Press, 1980.

Todd, Janet M. *The Secret Life of Aphra Behn*. Piscataway, NJ: Rutgers University Press, 1997.

BETTIGNIES, LOUISE DE *World War I*

Hoeling, A. A. *Women Who Spied*. New York: Madison Books, 1967.

Mahoney, M. H. *Women in Espionage, A Biographical Dictionary*. Santa Barbara, CA: ABC-CLIO, 1993.

Seth, Ronald. *Some of My Favorite Spies*. Philadelphia: Chilton Book Co., 1968.

BOWSER, MARY *The Civil War*

Allen, Thomas B. *Harriet Tubman, Secret Agent*. Washington, DC: National Geographic Society, 2006.

Jones, Katharine M. *Ladies of Richmond, Confederate Capital*. Indianapolis: Bobbs-Merrill, 1962.

MI Corps Hall of Fame. "Ms. Mary E. Bowser." *Military Intelligence Professional Bulletin*, July–September 1995.

Peterson, Harriette A. "Mary Elizabeth Bowser." In *Notable Black American Women*, edited by Jessie Carney Smith, 100–01. Detroit: Gale Research, 1992.

Varon, Elizabeth R. *Southern Lady, Yankee Spy: The True Story of Elizabeth Van Lew, A Union Agent in the Heart of the Confederacy.* New York: Oxford University Press, Inc., 2003.

Winkler, H. Donald. *Stealing Secrets: How a Few Daring Women Deceived Generals, Impacted Battles, and Altered the Course of the Civil War.* Naperville, IL: Cumberland House, 2010.

BOYD, BELLE *The Civil War*
Boyd, Belle. *Belle Boyd in Camp and Prison, Written by Herself*, edited by Curtis Carroll Davis. New York: Thomas Yoseloff, 1968.

Leonard, Elizabeth D. *All the Daring of the Soldier: Women of the Civil War Armies.* New York: W. W. Norton & Co., 1999.

Martini, Teri. *The Secret Is Out: True Spy Stories.* Boston: Little Brown, 1990.

CHILD, JULIA *World War II*
McIntosh, Elizabeth P. *Sisterhood of Spies: The Women of the OSS.* New York: Dell Publishing, 1998.

CODE BREAKERS *World War I*
National Security Agency. "Cryptologic Heritage: Women in American Cryptology." Accessed February 10, 2012. http://www.nsa.gov/about/cryptologic_heritage /women/index.shtml.

CUSHMAN, PAULINE *The Civil War*
Christen, William J. *Pauline Cushman: Spy of the Cumberland.* Roseville, MN: Edinborough Press, 2006.

Kane, Harnett T. *Spies for the Blue and Gray.* Garden City, NY: Hanover House, 1954.

Leonard, Elizabeth D. *All the Daring of the Soldier: Women of the Civil War Armies.* New York: W.W. Norton & Co., 1999

Sarmiento, Ferdinand L. *Life of Pauline Cushman.* Philadelphia: John E. Potter & Co., 1865.

US Department of Veterans Affairs. "Historical Information." Accessed November 28, 2011, http://www.cem.va.gov/cems/nchp/sanfrancisco.asp.

Winkler, H. Donald. *Stealing Secrets: How a Few Daring Women Deceived Generals, Impacted Battles, and Altered the Course of the Civil War.* Naperville, IL: Cumberland House, 2010.

DARRAGH, LYDIA *The American Revolution*
Bohrer, Melissa Lukeman. *Glory, Passion, and Principle: The Story of Eight Remarkable Women at the Core of the American Revolution.* New York: Atria Books, 2003.

Drinker, Sophie H. "Lydia Barrington Darragh." In *Notable American Women, 1607–1950: A Biographical Dictionary*, edited by Edward T. James, Janet Wilson James, and Paul Boyer, 434–35. Cambridge, MA: The Belknap Press of Harvard University Press, 1971.

Hoehling, A. A. *Women Who Spied: True Stories of Feminine Espionage.* New York: Dodd, Mead & Co., 1967.

Larson, Kate Clifford. *Bound for the Promised Land: Harriet Tubman, Portrait of an American Hero.* New York: W. W. Norton & Co., 1999.

Leonard, Elizabeth D. *All the Daring of the Soldier: Women of the Civil War Armies.* New York: W. W. Norton & Co., 1999.

Williams, Jean Kinney. *The Quakers.* Danbury, CT: Franklin Watts, 1998.

Zeinert, Karen. *Those Remarkable Women of the American Revolution.* Brookfield, CT: The Millbrook Press, 1996.

DE DOMINGUEZ, JOSEFA ORTIZ *The Wars of Independence in Spanish America*

Adams, Jerome R. *Notable Latin American Women: Twenty-nine Leaders, Rebels, Poets, Battlers and Spies, 1500–1900.* Jefferson, NC: McFarland & Co., 1995.

Anzures, Rafael. *Coleccion de biografías del los principales heroes de la independencia de Mexico.* Tlaxcala, Mexico: Oficina Tipográfica del Gobierno, 1909.

Chasteen, John Charles. *Americanos: Latin America's Struggle for Independence.* New York: Oxford University Press, Inc., 2008.

Gugliotta, Bobette. *Women of Mexico: The Consecrated and the Commoners, 1519–1900.* Encino, CA: Floricanto Press, 1989.

Sosa, Francisco. *Biografías de Mexicanos distinguidos.* Mexico City: Oficina Tipográfica de la Secretaría de Foment, 1884.

EDMONDS, SARAH EMMA *The Civil War*

Dannett, Sylvia G. L. *She Rode with the Generals: The True and Incredible Story of Sarah Emma Seelye, alias Franklin Thompson.* New York: Thomas Nelson & Sons, 1960.

Hall, Richard. *Patriots in Disguise: Women Warriors of the Civil War.* New York: Marlowe & Co., 1994.

Leonard, Elizabeth D. *All the Daring of the Soldier: Women of the Civil War Armies.* New York: W. W. Norton & Co., 1999.

Stevens, Bryna. *Frank Thompson: Her Civil War Story.* New York: Macmillan Publishers Co., 1992.

ELLIOTT, MABEL *World War I*

Coughlan, Sean. "Unknown Heroine Who Caught Invisible Ink Spy." *BBC News, Education and Family*, November 7, 2011. http://www.bbc.co.uk/news/education-15621443?print=true.

"World War I Spies Caught by Women Who Read Invisible Ink." *CBC News, Technology and Science*, November 10, 2011. http://www.cbc.ca/news/technology/story/2011/11/10/science-mabel-elliott-spies-royal-society.html.

GEIGER, EMILY *The American Revolution*

Bodie, Idella. *The Secret Message. Heroes and Heroines of the American Revolution*. Orangeburg, SC: Sandlapper Publishing, Inc., 1998.

Clark, Frank O. *Emily Geiger, a set of source documents*. Accessed February 28, 2012. http://sciway3.net/clark/revolutionarywar/geigeroutline.html.

Ellet, Elizabeth F. *Women of the American Revolution*, vol. 2. New York: Baker and Scribner, 1850.

Imrey, Harriet. Emails to Pamela D. Greenwood, November 6–9, 2002.

GULOVICH, MARIA *World War II*

Atwood, Kathryn J. *Women Heroes of World War II: 26 Stories of Espionage, Sabotage, Resistance, and Rescue*. Chicago: Chicago Review Press, 2011.

Downs, Jim. *World War II: OSS Tragedy in Slovakia*. Oceanside, CA: Liefrinck Publishers, 2002.

Liu, Maria Gulovich. Interview with Elizabeth G. Macalaster. Oxnard, CA. December 10, 2002.

McIntosh, Elizabeth P. *Sisterhood of Spies: The Women of the OSS*. New York: Dell Publishing, 1998.

HALL, VIRGINIA *World War II*

McIntosh, Elizabeth P. *Sisterhood of Spies: The Women of the OSS*. New York: Dell Publishing, 1998.

Pearson, Judith L. *The Wolves at the Door: The True Story of America's Greatest Female Spy*. Guilford, CT: The Globe Pequot Press, 2008.

Rossiter, Margaret L. *Women in the Resistance*. New York: Praeger, 1986.

HARRISON, MARGUERITE *World War I*

Mahoney, M. H. *Women in Espionage: A Biographical Dictionary*. Santa Barbara, CA: ABC-CLIO, 1993.

Olds, Elizabeth F. *Women of the Four Winds*. Boston: Houghton Mifflin Company, 1985.

KHAN, NOOR INAYAT AND NOOR'S JATAKA TALES *World War II*

Atwood, Kathryn J. *Women Heroes of World War II: 26 Stories of Espionage, Sabotage, Resistance, and Rescue*. Chicago: Chicago Review Press, 2011.

Basu, Shrabani. *Spy Princess: The Life of Noor Inayat Khan.* Stroud, Gloucestershire, UK: Sutton Publishing Limited, 2006.

Fuller, Jean Overton. *Madeleine: The Story of Noor Inayat Khan.* London: Victor Gollancz, Ltd., 1952.

Khan, Noor Inayat. *Twenty Jataka Tales.* Reprinted. Rochester, VT: Inner Traditions International, 1975.

LAMARR, HEDY *World War II*
"Female Inventors: Hedy Lamarr." *American Heritage of Invention and Technology,* 12, no. 4 (Spring 1997). http://www.inventions.org/culture/female/lamarr.html.

Ouellette, Jennifer. "Hop, Skip and a Jump: Remembering Hedy Lamarr." *Cocktail Party Physics* (blog), January 9, 2012. http://blogs.scientificamerican.com/cocktail -party-physics/2012/01/09/ hop-skip-and-a-jump-remembering-hedy-lamar/.

Rhodes, Richard. *Hedy's Folly: The Life and Breakthrough Inventions of Hedy Lamarr.* New York: Doubleday, 2011.

LANGSTON, LAODICEA *The American Revolution*
Bodie, Idella. *Spunky Revolutionary War Heroine. Heroes and Heroines of the American Revolution.* Orangeburg, SC: Sandlapper Publishing Co., Inc., 2000.

Ellet, Elizabeth F. *Women of the American Revolution,* vol. 1. New York: Baker and Scribner, 1850.

Imrey, Harriet. Emails to Pamela D. Greenwood, November 8–16, 2002.

Langston, EZ "Laodicea Langston: 'Daring Dicey.'" *Langston Ancestry Pages* (website). http://www.ezlangston.com/dicey.html.

LEGENDRE, GERTRUDE S. *World War II*
Legendre, Gertrude Sanford. *The Time of My Life.* Charleston, SC: Wyrick and Company, 1987.

———. *The Sands Ceased to Run.* New York: William Frederick Press, 1947.

MARBLE, ALICE *World War II*
Marble, Alice. *Courting Danger.* With Dale Leatherman. New York: St. Martin's Press. 1991.

Roger, Thomas. "Alice Marble, 77, Top U.S. Tennis Star of 1930s." *New York Times,* December 14, 1990: D23.

MATA HARI *see Zelle, Margaretha Geertruida*

MENDEZ, JONNA HIESTAND *The Cold War*
Mendez, Antonio, and Jonna Mendez. *Spy Dust: Two Masters of Disguise Reveal the Tools and Operations that Helped Win the Cold War.* With Bruce Henderson. New York: Atria Books, 2002.

Mendez, Jonna. Email to Elizabeth G. Macalaster, February 11, 2003.

MORAN, LINDSAY *A Changing World*

Ensor, David. "Moran: 'It's a Dirty Business.'" CNN. http://www.cnn.com/2005 /US/01/11/spy.life.

Kegley, Lindsay Moran. "Women in the CIA: Problems and Prospects." *UVA Top News Daily*, July 26, 2004. http://www.virginia.edu/topnews/07_26_2004/mcr_spy.html.

Moran, Lindsay. *Blowing My Cover: My Life as a CIA Spy*. New York: Berkley Books, 2005.

———. Email to Pamela D. Greenwood, December 30, 2011.

Parven, Cari Shane. "Lindsay Moran: CIA Spy Blowing My Cover." *Inside the Beltway, Under the Radar* (blog), January 23, 2008. http://insidethestory.net /print.php?getBlog=12.

PACK, BETTY *World War II*

Lovell, Mary S. *Cast No Shadow: the Life of the American Spy Who Changed the Course of World War II*. New York: Pantheon Books, 1992.

McIntosh, Elizabeth P. *Sisterhood of Spies: The Women of the OSS*. New York: Dell Publishing, 1998.

Sullivan, George. *In the Line of Fire: Eight Women War Spies*. New York: Scholastic, 1996.

RICHER, MARTHE *World War I*

Franklin, Charles. *The Great Spies*. New York: Hart Publishing, 1967.

Mahoney, M. H. *Women in Espionage: A Biographical Dictionary*. Santa Barbara, CA: ABC-CLIO, 1993.

"Marthe Betenfeld Richer." *The Penguin Biographical Dictionary of Women*. London: Penguin Books Ltd., 1998.

RIMINGTON, STELLA *The Cold War*

Kirby, Terry. "MI5 Edges Out of the Shadows." *The Independent*, July 17, 1993. http://www.independent.co.uk/news/mi5-edges-out-of-the-shadows-42-of -elite-security-service-officers-are-women--terrorists-are-main-target--bugging -of-royal-family-denied--booklet-outlines-organisation-1485397.html.

"Stella Rimington." *Gale Biography* in Context. February 29, 2012. http:// ic.galegroup.com/ic/bic1/ReferenceDetailsPage/ReferenceDetailsWindow?displ ayGroupName=Reference&disableHighlighting=false&prodId=BIC1&action=e&w indowstate=normal&catId=documentId=GALE%7CH1000151682&mode=view& userGroupName=ever29800&jsid=c94624d44c77fe611c0ce361cd4232ab

SALAVARRIETA, POLICARPA *The Wars of Independence in Spanish America*

Adams, Jerome R. *Notable Latin American Women: Twenty-nine Leaders, Rebels, Poets, Battlers and Spies, 1500–1900.* Jefferson, NC: McFarland & Co., 1995.

Chasteen, John Charles. *Americanos: Latin America's Struggle for Independence.* New York: Oxford University Press, Inc., 2008.

DuBois, Jill, and Leslie Jermyn. *Colombia.* Cultures of the World. Tarrytown, NY: Benchmark Books, 2002.

Earle, Rebecca A. *Spain and the Independence of Colombia, 1810–1825.* Exeter, UK: University of Exeter Press, 2000.

Henderson, James D., and Linda Roddy Henderson. *Ten Notable Women of Latin America.* Chicago: Nelson-Hall, 1978.

STORY, ANN *The American Revolution*

"Ann Reynolds Story." *Vermont Women's History Project* (website). Accessed November 18, 2011. http://womenshistory.vermont.gov/?TABID=61&personID=78.

Hahn, Michael T. *Ann Story: Vermont's Heroine of Independence.* Shelburne, VT: The New England Press, 1996.

Raabe, Emily. *Ethan Allen: The Green Mountain Boys and Vermont's Path to Statehood.* New York: The Rosen Publishing Group, Inc., 2002.

STRONG, ANNA SMITH *The American Revolution*

Currie, Catherine. *Anna Smith Strong and the Setauket Spy Ring.* Port Jefferson, NY: Precise Printing, Inc., 1992.

"Discover George Washington's Culper Spy Ring." *The Long Island North Shore Heritage Area* (website). Accessed February 28, 2012. http://linsha.org/spies.

Rose, Alexander. *Washington's Spies: The Story of America's First Spy Ring.* New York: Random House, Bantam Books, 2006.

"Spy Letters of the American Revolution." Collections of the Clements Library, University of Michigan, Ann Arbor, Michigan. Accessed February 28, 2012. http://www.clements.umich.edu/exhibits/online/spies/index-main2.html.

Tyler, Beverly C. "The Setauket Spies." E. Setauket, NY: Three Village Historical Society, 2005. Accessed February 28, 2012. http://www.three villagehistoricalsociety.org/18thcent.html.

SURRATT, MARY *The Civil War*

Larson, Kate Clifford. *The Assassin's Accomplice: Mary Surratt and the Plot to Kill Abraham Lincoln.* New York: Basic Books, 2008.

"Mrs. Surratt's Story," Surratt House Museum (website). August 24, 2010. Accessed December 12, 2011. http://www.surratt.org/su_hist.html.

Trindal, Elizabeth Steger. *Mary Surratt: An American Tragedy*. Gretna, LA: Pelican Publishing Company, 1996.

Winkler, H. Donald. *Stealing Secrets: How a Few Daring Women Deceived Generals, Impacted Battles, and Altered the Course of the Civil War*. Naperville, IL: Cumberland House, 2010.

TUBMAN, HARRIET *The Civil War*

Bradford, Sarah. *Harriet Tubman: The Moses of Her People*. Gloucester, MA: Peter Smith, 1981.

Davidson, Nancy A. "Harriet Tubman: 'Moses.'" In *Notable Black American Women*, edited by Jessie Carney Smith. Detroit: Gale Research, 1992.

Humez, Jean M. *Harriet Tubman: The Life and the Life Stories*. Madison: The University of Wisconsin Press, 2003.

Larson, Kate Clifford. *Bound for the Promised Land: Harriet Tubman, Portrait of an American Hero*. New York: Ballantine Books, 2004.

Taylor, M. W. *Harriet Tubman: Antislavery Activist*. Philadelphia: Chelsea House Publishers, 1991.

VAN LEW, ELIZABETH *The Civil War*

Allen, Thomas B. *Harriet Tubman, Secret Agent*. Washington, DC: National Geographic Society, 2006.

Beymer, William Gilmore. *On Hazardous Service: Scouts and Spies of the North and South*. New York: Harper & Brothers Publishers, 1912.

Van Lew, Elizabeth. *A Yankee Spy in Richmond: The Civil War Diary of "Crazy Bet" Van Lew*, edited by David D. Ryan. Mechanicsburg, PA: Stackpole Books, 1996.

Varon, Elizabeth R. *Southern Lady, Yankee Spy: The True Story of Elizabeth Van Lew, A Union Agent in the Heart of the Confederacy*. New York: Oxford University Press, 2003.

Winkler, H. Donald. *Stealing Secrets: How a Few Daring Women Deceived Generals, Impacted Battles, and Altered the Course of the Civil War*. Naperville, IL: Cumberland House, 2010.

Zeinert, Karen. *Elizabeth Van Lew: Southern Belle, Union Spy*. Parsippany, NJ: Dillon Press, 1995.

VICARIO, LEONA *The Wars of Independence in Spanish America*

Adams, Jerome R. *Notable Latin American Women: Twenty-nine Leaders, Rebels, Poets, Battlers and Spies, 1500–1900*. Jefferson, NC: McFarland & Co., 1995.

Anzures, Rafael. *Coleccion de biografías del los principales heroes de la independencia de Mexico*. Tlaxcala Mexico: Oficina Tipográfica del Gobierno, 1909.

Chasteen, John Charles. *Americanos: Latin America's Struggle for Independence*. New York: Oxford University Press, Inc., 2008.

Gugliotta, Bobette. *Women of Mexico: The Consecrated and the Commoners, 1519–1900*. Encino, CA: Floricanto Press, 1989.

Sosa, Francisco. *Biografías de Mexicanos distinguidos*. Mexico City: Oficina Tipográfica de la Secretaría de Foment, 1884.

WARD, NANYE'HI (NANCY) *The American Revolution*

Berkin, Carol. *Revolutionary Mothers: Women in the Struggle for America's Independence*. New York: Alfred A. Knopf, 2005.

Bohrer, Melissa Lukeman. *Glory, Passion, and Principle: The Story of Eight Remarkable Women at the Core of the American Revolution*. New York: Atria Books, 2003.

WILSON, VALERIE PLAME *A Changing World*

Pincus, Walter and Mike Allen. "Damage from Spy Leak Widens as CIA Front Company Has Its Cover Blown." *The Sydney Morning Herald*, October 6, 2003. http://www.smh.com.au/articles/2003/10/05/106529.

Wilson, Valerie Plame. *Fair Game: My Life as a Spy, My Betrayal by the White House*. New York: Simon and Schuster, 2007.

WRIGHT, PATIENCE *The American Revolution*

Sellers, Charles Coleman. *Patience Wright: American Artist and Spy in George III's London*. Middletown, CT: Wesleyan University Press, 1976.

Shea, Pegi Deitz. *Patience Wright: America's First Sculptor and Revolutionary Spy*. New York: Henry Holt and Company, 2007.

WU, EVA *The Chinese Revolution*

Mahoney, M. H. *Women in Espionage: A Biographical Dictionary*. Santa Barbara, CA: ABC-CLIO, 1993.

Singer, Kurt. *Spy Stories from Asia*. New York: Wilfred Funk, Inc., 1955.

ZELLE, MARGARETHA GEERTRUIDA (MATA HARI) *World War I*

Howe, Russell Warren. *Mata Hari, the True Story*. New York: Dodd, Mead & Co., 1986.

Shipman, Pat. *Femme Fatale: Love, Lies, and the Unknown Life of Mata Hari*. New York: William Morrow, 2007.

SPY FILES

Brackman, Barbara. *Facts and Fabrications: Unraveling the History of Quilts and Slavery.* Lafayette, CA: C&T Publishing, 2006.

Danigelis, Alyssa. "10 Trickiest Spy Gadgets Ever." *Discovery Tech* (website). Accessed March 7, 2012. http://dsc.discovery.com/technology/tech-10 /spy-gadgets-top-10.html.

McKay, Brett, and Kate McKay. "Man Knowledge: 15 Cool Spy Concealments." *The Art of Manliness* (blog). November 15, 2011. Accessed March 7, 2012. http:// artofmanliness.com/2011/11/15/man-knowledge-15-cool-spy-concealments/.

Mendez, Tony, and Jonna Mendez website. Accessed March 7, 2012. http:// www.themasterofdisguise.com/.

National Museum of the American Indian website. Accessed January 3, 2012. http://www.nmai.si.edu/.

Owen, David. *Hidden Secrets: A Complete History of Espionage and the Technology Used to Support It.* Toronto: Firefly Books, 2002.

Platt, Richard. *Eyewitness: Spy.* New York: DK Publishing, 2000.

Windrem, Rober. "Spy Satellites Enter New Dimension." MSNBC, August 8, 1998. http://www.msnbc.com/id/3077885/ns/technology.